Praise for Take Control of the Noisy Class

In a clear, reassuring, no-nonsense tone, Rob Plevin shows how our attitudes and expectations as teachers translate into a simple set of routines that can make all the difference. His guidance is easy to implement, unpatronising and hugely optimistic – because once behaviour expectations are clearly bedded-in, we can get to the heart of our role – teaching our students. *Take Control of the Noisy Class* helps us to do just what the title promises. I strongly recommend it.

Geoff Barton, General Secretary, ASCL

Rob has written the kind of book that every teacher – regardless of experience – will learn something from. Underpinned with lively stories, anecdotes, illustrations and pertinent theory, this book will make any teacher who has ever struggled with an unruly class or troublesome student feel that they now have the understanding and tools to solve their own classroom problems. Highly recommend.

Isabella Wallace, teacher, author and education consultant

Plevin's text is written in the inimitable style loved by his website fans. His sage advice and how-to-do-it strategies are passed onto readers with the good natured, quirky, self-deprecating humour for which he is known. He writes to us in language reminiscent of a vivid collegial conversation in the teachers' lunchroom. It's very much like having a friendly, funny conversation with a deeply thoughtful master teacher.

Dr Tom McIntyre, BehaviorAdvisor.com,
professor, Hunter College, City University of New York

I had expected to skim this book but was completely unable to do so. The writing style is incredibly engaging. The stories Rob tells pull you in: not only to understand his thought process, but to create effective analogies so that the reader can completely understand his points.

While I read this book, I wanted to shout from the rooftop, 'Yes, yes, yes!' If every classroom teacher used these strategies and techniques in their classroom, they would definitely be able to take control of a noisy class.

Susan Fitzell, author, education consultant and professional speaker

Imagine having quick and easy-to-use strategies to calm your class in just 15 seconds! How I wish I'd had these strategies when I first began to teach. One that I especially love builds on leadership roles with the students who are typically the loudest and trains them in how to immediately quieten the class. As with every strategy in this crucially important book, it's brilliant, practical and works right away. Rob, you've done a remarkable service for teachers and students alike. The 'quiet' in the classroom transforms student behaviour as well as the learning process. Thank you!

Pat Wyman, MA, author of *Amazing Grades* and founder, HowToLearn.com

Rob Plevin's new book combines my two favourite elements of a teaching resource: useable, practical ideas presented in an easy-to-read style. These down-to-earth, sensible strategies will be immediately useful to educators working with students of any age. Buy it, read it, and start stealing ideas today!

Dr Rich Allen, greenlighteducation.net

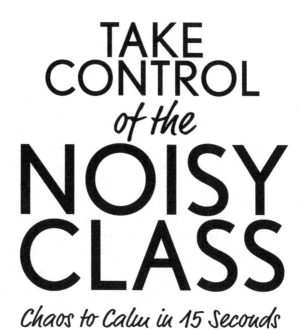

TAKE
CONTROL
of the
NOISY
CLASS

Chaos to Calm in 15 Seconds

ROB PLEVIN

LIFERAFTMEDIA Ltd
www.liferaftmedia.com

Published by
Life Raft Media Ltd
www.liferaftmedia.com

Copyright Rob Plevin 2018

Print ISBN: 978-1-9993451-0-5
Kindle ISBN: 978-1-9993451-1-2
eBook/Other: 978-1-9993451-2-9

I would like to dedicate this book to my parents – for their love and support and for the fact that no matter how I have behaved throughout my life, they never stopped believing in me.

And also to my wonderful partner, Sally, and my amazing children, Joe, Andrew and Poppy. Thanks gang – I am filled with gratitude for the joy, laughter and learning you bring to my life each day.

Acknowledgements

I am indebted to my good friend Adam Page for his help with this book, and indeed all my materials. He has put up with my last minute, unrealistic deadlines for years.

Thanks to Bob, my first mentor, 'Boss Woman' Susan, Gail and Shay – some of the best strategies in this book came from them during the roller-coaster time we spent together in Gateshead. Thanks also to all the kids I've worked with over the years – most of the remaining strategies came about through trying to avoid the stress they were causing me!

Contents

Introduction

Once upon a time, a fresh-faced, idealistic young teacher emerged blinking from teacher training camp. Armed only with a dream of putting the education world to rights, brand new elbow patches and a burning ambition to be the most popular teacher in school, he tackled the world head on. He challenged the establishment and won. He changed the face of education forever. The kids loved him, his results were outstanding and Benedict Cumberbatch won an Oscar for playing him in the film. And then I woke up.

I have to admit I found the real teaching world a bit of a shock and came down to earth with a bump. Dealing with teenagers who didn't want to be in school wasn't easy and I soon realised how ill-equipped I was in terms of practical classroom management strategies. I'll be honest and tell you I *really* struggled with some students and I was pathetic at keeping the more challenging groups under control.

To be fair, it was the same story for most other members of staff. This was a tough school, but even so, there were still one or two exceptions who seemed to have the respect and adulation of even the hardest students. These were the teachers the kids adored. When they walked down a corridor the students would make a beeline for them to say hello and have a chat, the mood in their classroom was almost always upbeat and as soon as they began to teach a respectful hush would immediately descend. 'That is the kind of teacher I want to be!' I thought. Now to find out how they do it …

I found that the simplest way was to ask them – the students, that is, not the teachers. I wanted to hear *them* tell me what it was they wanted to see in a teacher. So, over the years and in several different settings, I compiled questionnaires for my classes, of all ages between 7 and 18, designed to root out the answer to that one big question: what makes the best teacher you've ever met?

I used the questionnaires to probe deeper than that, of course. I wanted to know what these teachers said, what they did, what teaching methods they used, what strategies they employed to help kids when they were down, how they used humour in the classroom, how they encouraged the students to work harder, how they got them to follow instructions, what they did that made them smile.

Call me obsessive (I've had worse) but there was a hidden agenda. I had watched these individuals in action for some time before it hit me: these teachers were enjoying their careers far more than their peers. The teaching day wasn't a grind to them. It wasn't the gruelling endurance test that some teachers would have me believe. Here were teachers who enjoyed coming to school to teach students who enjoyed being taught.

I wanted to be one of these teachers, not the jaded moaner grumbling into his coffee in the corner of the staffroom every breaktime. And that is why I spent so much time questioning my students. The results won't surprise you, as they didn't surprise me. All the expected criteria were there. The following list (in no particular order) represents the features that the students said they most wanted to see in their 'best teacher'.

- They treat us in a friendly manner.

- They acknowledge when we do something right.

- They know how to have a laugh.

- They give out information in a fun and interesting way.

- They trust us.

- They are firm and fair, with the same rules for all.

- They are always in control.

- They are there for us, they care, they listen.

As I said, no surprises, yet it took me a long time to realise just how important this short list really is and why it embodies the key to both preventing and dealing with behaviour problems in the classroom. You see, after years of compiling my little questionnaires, it dawned on me that the reason these teachers were having such an easy time in the classroom wasn't only because they provided interesting lessons and were firm and fair. There is an important reason why the essential attributes listed above, taken as a whole, are so effective in preventing problems and helping students feel content: they satisfy three crucial human needs.

You'll no doubt be familiar with Abraham Maslow's hierarchy of needs theory. It suggests that all humans share basic needs and that once a group of needs is met or satisfied, we move up to the next level. The lowest level consists of our most basic needs – shelter, food, water and safety. Then we progress into the realms of a wide range of emotional and psychological needs – from the need to achieve through to the need to contribute, the need for love and a whole host of others in-between. These needs must be met in order for us to feel content and whole.

I like things to be simple so I've lumped into three groups what I feel to be the most important of the psychological needs in terms of classroom management. The first group falls under the heading of *empowerment* and includes things like recognition, freedom, autonomy, achievement, contribution, choice and competence. Second is the need for *fun*, which includes curiosity, interest, growth and learning, adventure, amusement, surprise and variety. Finally, there is the need to *belong* – to be accepted, valued, appreciated, needed, related to or connected with something beyond oneself.

If you think about this it makes perfect sense. We humans don't function well without adequate control, choice, autonomy and freedom in our lives – we need to be empowered. We can't live happy lives without at least some variety, humour, activity or fun. And we feel isolated and alone if we're not valued or appreciated by others or connected to them in some way – we need to belong. When these three needs are not being met – when they are missing from our lives – we feel frustrated and discontented. And that's when the problems start.

Consider the following scenario: imagine a thoroughly boring lesson. You know the type I mean – a teacher handing out worksheet after worksheet, standing at the front of the room, talking like a shop window dummy going through the motions. There is no engaging warm-up activity to grab the students' attention, no variety or choice in terms of lesson tasks or level of challenge, no novelty or intrigue, no humour, no laughter, no sense of discovery, no interaction or movement around the room, no music, no curiosity, no energy, no recognition or praise for efforts made and no attention given to differing learning styles. It's the kind of lesson that makes kids want to get up and walk out.

What usually happens in a lesson like this? You guessed it: students misbehave.

It might start with fairly innocent activities such as doodling or passing notes, but left unchecked these activities become increasingly disruptive: getting up and walking around, throwing things, shouting silly comments, dishing out abuse to the teacher, not doing work, tapping pencils, refusing to follow instructions, dictating their own terms, using mobile phones and so on. What results is the typical behaviour problems arising from frustration and dissatisfaction – from needs that have not been met.

Remember, our psychological needs are crucial to us and must be satisfied – they are a primeval, subconscious thirst which must be quenched and are as important to us as water and sunlight are to a plant. If the teacher doesn't provide a means to meet these needs as part of regular day-to-day practice, then students will seek satisfaction in less appropriate ways of their own devising.

In other words, if you don't give them fun, they will make their own. If you don't give them a sense of empowerment, they will assert themselves in their own way. And if you don't help them feel valued, they will opt out and form troublemaking splinter groups. (Have you ever wondered why gangs are so appealing to young people?)

Throughout this book I will present some ways of satisfying these three key needs in order to help you prevent and deal with a large proportion of problems in your classroom. I call the underlying framework the Needs Focused Approach™, for obvious reasons. I don't claim that *all* your problems will be solved, but by adopting the strategies and ideas that follow you will definitely see a dramatic reduction in the number of incidents you are currently dealing with on a daily basis. And I guarantee that if you start to adopt some of the key principles, you will start to see big improvements in your ability to deal with any problems which do occur.

We are going to look at ways of helping students experience a sense of belonging by helping them feel part of the classroom community and by building positive, mutually respectful teacher–student bonds. It makes a huge difference to struggling, troubled (and troublesome) students to feel accepted, welcomed and valued in school.

We will look at ways of empowering students by providing them with realistic chances to achieve and experience success, by giving them a degree of autonomy and choice and by ensuring their efforts are recognised and acknowledged. Again, this comes down to helping students feel valued as well as giving them confidence in their abilities to attempt and complete lesson tasks.

And we will look at ways of improving lessons by making them more interactive and appealing, more stimulating, more relevant to students' lives and more fun. Now and again you can be forgiven for having a lesson of book work or worksheets. Now and again you can be forgiven for a lacklustre performance and for not displaying your usual enthusiasm and love for your subject. No problem there, that's life. The problems arise when the majority of lessons all follow the same format. If there is a continuing lack of challenge, variety and novelty, there will almost certainly be a continuing lack of interest from the students.

As well as all these preventive tools, strategies and ideas for maintaining a positive lesson environment, you are also going to learn a wide range of very practical, highly effective responses to use when things go wrong. You will get some ideas for consequences which actually work, together with a method for issuing them which doesn't lead to confrontation. You will find new ways to help students follow your instructions and you will have a suite of proven strategies for addressing many of the specific behaviour issues you are likely to face in today's tough classrooms. Finally, in Part 2, we will go through a complete, step-by-step sample lesson with the noisy class – from getting them into the room, settled and ready to work, to dismissing them with a smile.

What I've learned is that you really *can* succeed with the most challenging, noisy, rowdy and difficult groups of students. You really can gain the respect of antisocial, hard-to-reach teens and children. You can get them following your instructions without arguments and without fuss. You can have them arriving at your classroom with a smile and joining in lessons with enthusiasm – no matter how unresponsive or sullen they currently appear. And you really can enjoy stress-free, rewarding teaching – no matter how worn out and drained you feel right now and no matter how far-fetched that seems.

Best of all, these changes can happen quickly. I believe *any* teacher can succeed with practically *any* group of students if they employ certain key strategies with the right attitude and approach. Why? Because I've been exactly where you are now and I know how it feels to struggle in the classroom.

At the start of my teaching career I used to go home in the evenings in a rage, so angry that my students could get away with the things they did, furious that there seemed to be no way of reaching and dealing with them. They didn't respond to staff who were pleasant to them and they laughed in the faces of staff who tried to discipline them. Nothing seemed to work.

I couldn't sleep, I had a constant headache and I was on edge all the time. I worried what my colleagues thought of me and I dreaded teaching certain groups because I knew they would walk all over me. How embarrassing. How humiliating. I became bad tempered at home and all my conversations with friends centred around the horrors I was facing at work on a daily basis. Eventually, I began to look for other jobs. I became resigned to the fact that I didn't have what it took to work in tough schools with tough kids. My dream was over.

Then, by chance, things changed. I became a supply teacher while I looked for a way out and took a job for one afternoon at a pupil referral unit (PRU). The unit had recently been placed in special measures and it was easy to see why. I was shocked to see kids literally running wild through the corridors, slamming doors, ripping books, screaming and shouting abuse, running into the car park and throwing stones at the building. And all of this was happening *during* lesson time. Most of the staff had no control whatsoever and some were in tears.

But I was hooked. The children here fascinated me as much as their backgrounds horrified me. I started to see that there were reasons for the way they behaved. It was no wonder that nothing seemed to work – most of the strategies I had been using took no account of the issues and problems they faced. I decided there and then that I wanted to really connect with these young people. I wanted to help them succeed and I wanted to learn the skills that would enable me to manage their behaviour. I ended up staying for more than five years and enjoyed some of the most thorough and in-depth professional training any teacher could hope for in the field of behaviour management. It was tough, but I consider myself so fortunate for that experience.

Many of the ideas in this book come from my time spent in PRUs and behaviour units where the behaviour of students is incredibly demanding and needs the kind of management which would be deemed disproportionate or unnecessary in other settings. You may therefore feel that some of the strategies would be impractical for your classes. It all depends on your particular circumstances, of course – the institution, the age group, your subject and the type of students in your care. What works in some classrooms will not necessarily work in others. My intention is to provide you with a wide range of ideas which you can dip into and use as you see fit – it is not necessary to follow every single step in a prescriptive manner in order to benefit.

It is also my aim to help you begin to enjoy teaching again by eliminating some of the stress associated with tough students and by giving you the confidence and skills to calmly succeed with any group you teach. These strategies have the potential to create swift improvements in your ability to manage student behaviour and big improvements in the way uncooperative and obstinate students respond to you.

 Throughout the book you'll notice this little symbol popping up from time to time. It's there to let you know that there are additional resources available on a web page I've set up for you at www.noisyclass. com/bookresources. There's no charge for this – the resources come free with the book.

So, with the introduction out of the way, let's try out a quick strategy before we really get into the nitty-gritty …

How to get the noisy class quiet in 15 seconds

Not only can this technique get a group of students quiet in as little as a few seconds, it also strengthens teacher–student relationships, injects some humour into the session and gives challenging students the attention they crave. It also works equally well with 8-year-olds, 18-year-olds and even 63-year-olds (I haven't gone higher than that!). Indeed, I tried this at a recent teacher training seminar in Dubai and overheard one of the participants remarking, 'He just got a room of 150 rowdy people quiet in 15 seconds!'

It relies on two key principles: responsibilities and routines. Some of your students will respond very well to being given a responsibility. In fact, it's probably your most challenging students – the ringleaders – who will respond best to responsibility because they crave attention. A great way to give them this attention (in a very positive way) is to give them a job, and for this classroom strategy we are going to award three or four students with the job of getting the rest of the class quiet. These students are going to be our 'shushers' and it is their responsibility to 'shush' the rest of the class members (in a special way) when asked to do so.

To give them every chance of success we are going to train them. Each nominated shusher is asked to give their best and loudest shush – complete with an angry scowl and finger-on-lip gesture. After a few practices, the shushers are then told that whenever the teacher shouts out 'Shushers!' they are to give their best and loudest shush in unison. The rest of the class are told that when they hear the shushers shush they must stop talking and sit in

silence. After two or three practices they all get the idea and we now have the makings of a very effective routine in place.

To give the shushing routine the best chance of success there are three additions which I have found to be useful. First, your shushers need regular feedback. They should be told when they are doing a good job and given hints and pointers when they are slacking or messing around. Remember that the students you use as shushers are likely to be natural livewires so they will need careful management to make sure they continue to perform well. Ideally, any constructive feedback or corrective instructions should be given quietly and out of earshot of other students.

Second, I like to give each of my shushers a uniform to wear so they can be easily identified. The 'uniform' is actually just a silly hat or joke school cap, but they love wearing it, although I'm not entirely sure why. Maybe it helps them feel special, maybe it just makes the whole affair less serious, but whatever the reason, it seems to work.

Finally, I have found that shushers sometimes need a little extra help to get a particularly rowdy class to settle. I give them this by using another routine prior to calling on them – the countdown. This is simply the process of counting down slowly from 10 to 1 out loud, while giving encouragement along the way.

10 ... Okay everyone, by the time I get down to 1 you should all be sitting on your own seats with your bags away and your hands on the table ... Excellent Carly and Sophie, you got it straight away.

9 ... Brilliant over here on this table – let's have the rest of you doing the same.

8 ... You need to finish chatting, get that mess away and be sitting facing me.

7 ... All done over there at the back, well done. Just waiting for a few others.

6 ... Come on, still some bags out at the back and people talking.

5 ... Good.

4 ...

3 ...   We're just waiting for one group now. Ah, you've got it now and you're sitting perfectly, thank you.

2 ...   Well done everyone, nearly there ...

1 ...   Brilliant.

(Pause)

Shushers!

By the time you reach 1, most of your students will be settled and responsive, leaving the shushers to deal with the small minority who are still talking. Obviously, you can shorten the countdown, or even disregard it completely, if a group is relatively settled. At these times, the shushers alone can bring silence to your room.

So there you have it. A great way to get rowdy groups of students settled in record time. Now we can begin ...

Part 1

Establishing and maintaining control

Chapter 1
Classroom management essentials

Attitude is everything

Your attitude underpins everything you do. It determines the way you speak to students, the type of activities and tasks you offer them, the amount of time you allocate to building relationships with them and everything else besides. Your attitude is betrayed by the way you walk, the way you talk and the expression you wear when you meet students in the corridor or introduce your lessons.

In terms of managing behaviour your attitude is crucial. It will determine whether you use your ineffective *reactive* toolbox (comprising of emotional outbursts, threats, reprimands, dismissive comments and over-the-top punishments) or your highly effective *response* toolbox. This includes a range of more supportive, considered and helpful solutions which convey a level of care and compassion. You don't have to be a rocket scientist to guess which approach the students prefer and respond to best.

When encountering a boy ambling down the corridor with his shirt hanging out, teacher A might scream at him and threaten him with a detention, teacher B pretends to ignore him fearing a backlash he or she would struggle to deal with, while teacher C gives him a knowing smile and calmly tells him to tuck his shirt back in. Each of these teachers may well share the same opinion of the school rules but they treat students who break them differently. Their actions are determined by their *attitude*.

Teacher A (the bully) and teacher B (the wallflower) see challenging students as a threat – to their leadership, to the school, to their reputation, perhaps even to decent society. They tend to be problem focused and their attitude is largely negative. Empathy for our more challenging children lies at the heart of changing attitudes towards them and teacher C knows this is a boy 'with problems' rather than 'a problem boy'. He sees the situation as an opportunity to strengthen teacher–student relationships instead of a deliberate attempt to flout school rules.

Telling Jonny to 'get on with his work' is a typical stock response when he is messing around, but it doesn't address the underlying reasons why he's off task and therefore doesn't usually change his behaviour – certainly not for long. He might get his head down while you stand over him, but as soon as your back is turned he will revert to carving his name in the desk. Unless the underlying issue has been addressed, mindless vandalism will be infinitely more interesting than the worksheet you have given him.

If you are faced with students who flatly refuse to get started, who are constantly chatting, who are totally uninterested in the exciting task put before them or who turn up to class two days late, it is best to try to find the reason why this might be happening before trying to stop it happening again.

Here are a few possibilities to think about:

- Students who mess around and act the fool may simply want attention.

- Students who avoid work could be frustrated because the work is too difficult for them and they may feel they are getting left behind.

- Students who are huffy and argumentative may believe they are being picked on because they are being watched so closely and are therefore 'expected' to do something wrong.

- Students who opt out completely could have a lack of self-belief – convinced there is no point in trying after years of failure.

- Students who are disruptive may be bored – they may crave the variety, stimulation and challenge that the lesson isn't giving them.

- Students who are angry and abusive may resent past treatment which they see as unfair.

Of course, these are just possible reasons for the many incidents of inappropriate behaviour we see every day in tough classrooms. There could be all manner of explanations for why a student might not be settling as quickly as he should. It could be an issue at home, a bullying incident, worries about the work, a personality clash with another member of staff or a lack of clear boundaries in the classroom, to name but a few. One thing is for certain – there is *always* a reason behind the behaviour we see. It is not just blatant belligerence. Knowing and remembering this is vitally important because it will change our attitude towards these students and determine the plan and strategies we use to deal with the resulting behaviours.

Tough students hate teachers who aren't sensitive to their problems. If they don't respond immediately with a mouthful of abuse (or worse) on the spot, they will certainly harbour resentment which will only lead to confrontation further down the line. And remember this too: most groups of young people will take sides with any student they perceive to have been unfairly treated by an angry teacher, even if that student is not particularly popular or well-liked. It's down to the 'them and us' undercurrent in most schools, and the teacher who forgets this will suddenly find himself dealing with 35 challenging students instead of just one.

Early on in my own career I tore strips off a 15-year-old boy called Steven who arrived to class 15 minutes late and rudely interrupted my science lesson. It was my first day at a new school and I was very pleased with myself – I think I may have even puffed my chest out – when he eventually followed my bellowed command to remove himself from the classroom. I conducted the rest of the lesson with a swagger.

Later that day a senior colleague took me aside and told me about some of the emotional pressures that poor boy was facing at home. It was no wonder that he was causing problems at school. At lunchtime I tracked him down so that I could apologise to him, and I was surprised how well he responded to this change in approach. I returned home that day with tears in my eyes.

For years Steven sprang into my mind whenever I was confronted by a student who I assumed was being deliberately belligerent or non-compliant. He taught me the valuable lesson that there are always reasons behind bad behaviour. This doesn't mean we teachers need the full background on every student we encounter before we can make headway. It's not necessary for us to be privy to every student's home life or individual set of difficult circumstances. We just need to remember that young people often act the way they do because of issues they are facing or carrying. Their behaviour is more often a cry for help than a personal attack.

With empathy comes a total change in the way we view these young people and a total change in our attitude towards them. And with this shift in viewpoint comes a change in the tools we use to manage them. We will be looking at a range of very effective, non-confrontational strategies for your response toolbox throughout the rest of this book.

Be vigilant – what you miss persists

Sometimes there is so much going on in the classroom that you might fail to spot a note being passed around, or you might miss some low level verbal bullying or items being stolen or broken. Your eyes can't be everywhere at once and it is understandable that some incidents go unnoticed.

However, every time a student gets away with passing a note, calling someone an offensive name, writing on the desk or nicking your wallet, you are effectively encouraging them to do the same again. Every time teachers fail to act when a student 'forgets' to bring a pen to class, arrives late or interrupts the lesson flow, we give the clear message that they can do as they please – and get away with it. And it doesn't stop there either, because it's not just the perpetrator who will repeat the action. Other students who witness these behaviours going unchallenged will feel they can do the same too.

A lack of vigilance can create an environment where 'anything goes', and once this takes root in your classroom these problem behaviours become more and more common and get harder and harder to stamp out. The only way to prevent this is to be more attentive and to jump on any problem as soon as possible. After all, it is much easier dealing with problems when they are small – before they become established.

So how does this work in practice? Well, if you see two students starting to bicker, give them a warning or separate them – quickly. If a student is starting to get wound up, offer him some support – quickly. If a student is becoming bored or has finished his work and is starting to fidget, change the level of challenge or give him something else to do – quickly. Pay attention to these warning signs and act on them before they escalate. Challenge rule breakers every time (even those students you would rather not confront because they are prone to retaliate fiercely) and make sure your presence is felt in every area of the room. Be constantly on the move, teach from each corner of the room, walk around the tables and speak to all the students. Let them know this is your room, that you really do have eyes in the back of your head and you are aware of everything that is going on.

I've observed struggling teachers who seem to spend the entire lesson in a tiny area at the front of the room. By simply moving around the room more, walking to the back when addressing the group or spending a few moments offering friendly support and checking the work of students you normally avoid, you will be amazed how the atmosphere in the room changes. When you act as though you own the room – all of it – you will see an immediate and marked decrease in the amount of disruptive behaviour you have to deal with.

Remain calm

Whenever we go steaming in to 'sort out' a student, we run the risk of making the situation far worse because we are fighting fire with fire. A calm, matter-of-fact approach is far more effective than shrieking. Shouting gives the impression that you have lost control so keep the emotional outbursts for the times they have done something right. If you have a penchant for standing on the table and shouting, do it when Jonny has finished his first essay, by way of celebration, and not in response to him calling you a 'fat ****'.

Keeping calm is also about not getting drawn into students' backchat or attempts to start an argument with you, no matter how much eye rolling, muttering, complaining and swearing they try. This will not only give them the reaction they are trying to provoke but you also run the risk of the situation escalating into a much more serious incident. Once they get you started, they really don't like the show to end.

Make your interventions less disruptive than the behaviour you're targeting (aka the law of least intervention)

Imagine you have 35 students in your classroom, each working quietly with their heads down, but one student at the back of the room is off task. This one individual, our old friend Jonny, isn't doing anything particularly disruptive *yet*, but clearly you need to get him on task quickly before his behaviour escalates and he does do something to attract the attention of the other students.

An inexperienced teacher might call out to him and tell him to get on with his work: 'Jonny, stop burning your book and get on with your work, please!' It's a reasonable response. But what will happen now? Instead of one student off task there are now 35 students off task, all very interested in what Jonny will do next and how the teacher is going to deal with it.

The law of least intervention states that we should always use the least intrusive or least disruptive method of dealing with a student so that we don't disturb and/ or attract the attention of other students in the room. This also means we avoid having the flow of the lesson disrupted. A student who is late, for example, should be quietly directed to a vacant seat (a simple hand gesture is all that is needed), given work to get on with and then spoken with at the end of the lesson when the audience has left the room. In private you can calmly ask them if there was a valid reason for them being late and deal with them accordingly if not. (For more strategies see 'Dealing with latecomers and poor punctuality' on page 240.) And a child who is chewing gum in your room should be tactically ignored at first and then dealt with when the rest of the group is busy. At that point you could nonchalantly take the bin to them and point to it or quietly ask them to put the gum in it.

In both cases, this approach is much better than making a spectacle out of a kid who is breaking the rules – you'll either embarrass them and cause them to retaliate or you'll give them the audience they want. We all like to show off when we're good at something and kids who are good at being argumentative like nothing more than to argue and stand up to you when their mates are watching.

Be consistent

All students – those you are dealing with, as well as those watching you deal with them – need to see you being consistent. They need to know that you will deal with anyone who is not doing what they should be every time they are not doing it and that you will treat everyone the same. Letting Chantelle wear her headphones – because she has an awful temper and really kicks off when challenged – sends a clear signal to her (and her friends) that she can wear them again next lesson, as can the six others who saw her get away with it. When you bend the rules for one, you create a rod for your own back.

In every classroom situation there are going to be students who push boundaries too far no matter how positive and student centred you are. Some won't respect a teacher who is too 'nice'. Some are intent on ruining a lesson however engaging and exciting you have made the tasks. Some think any teacher who doesn't have tattoos is a pushover. These are all reasons why a system of stepped consequences (which we'll come to in Chapter 4) is essential.

But remember: it's the way you apply these consequences that affects their success – you have to be consistent in every aspect. You can't use them one day and not the next. You can't apply them to one student and not his friend. You can't apply them with a patronising sneer to one student and an apologetic wince to another. You must do what you say you are going to do in the same way every time.

If your rule on not finishing work in class is that students have to return at break-time or stay behind after school for ten minutes to finish it, then it *must* happen. If you don't chase up the no-shows then you may as well not bother with having the rule in the first place. Yes, chasing up the detention dodgers will be time consuming, but only in the short term.

It's a case of short term pain for long term gain, but struggling teachers usually take the opposite route. They give in to students who whine and complain. They let students off despite having given them a warning. They make repeated warnings but never actually follow through on them. They give over-the-top threats which make it difficult to follow through anyway. They choose to look the other way or ignore certain students when they break the rules because they know that challenging them will result in an outburst or confrontation which they fear they won't be able to control.

So, in the short term they take what they think to be the easy, pain free route. Just like the parent in the supermarket who buys their screaming toddler the very item they were adamant they couldn't have just two minutes ago. In doing so they unwittingly set themselves up for a world of problems. When we opt for short term pain for long term gain it can seem as if we're making no progress at first, and there may even be an increase in bad behaviour as students buck against the new system you're imposing. But stick with it – the rewards are huge for the consistent teacher.

If you have to take the class back out of the room because they won't listen to you, do so. If you have to have them practise lining up at the door for the entire lesson because they won't follow your instructions to the letter, do so. And if you then have to bring them back at breaktime or lunchtime to practise until they see that you mean business, then this is what you must do. It might mean liaising with form tutors or heads of year. It might mean making countless phone calls home or even embarking on home visits. But all this legwork builds your reputation, and once they get the fact that you don't give in – that you follow up every time – you will start to *save* time. Eventually, I promise you, they will get the message and see that it is easier for them to do as you ask.

Be respectful: the way we respond will determine how they react

There are two ways of dealing with students who aren't behaving as we want them to – fairly and unfairly. Not surprisingly, it doesn't matter what our idea of 'fair' is; it's what they think that counts.

Embarrassing them, picking on them, scolding them and shouting at them will be considered unfair, obviously, and will result in stress, arguments and tantrums. But in some cases a student will feel equally persecuted just by the way we speak to them or even just the way we're looking at them – as we all know, body language and facial expressions play a huge part in communication. On more than one occasion I've witnessed a student launching into a full physical assault on a member of staff for nothing more than a raised eyebrow yelling, 'I f****** hate you! I hate the way you look at me!'

Young people are experts at reading our inner feelings but they have little control over their own emotions, so when they believe that we dislike them or have something against them then their reactions can often seem extreme. And when a whole group of students feel we are being confrontational or unfair, the problem suddenly becomes about 35 times worse.

If we minimise or eliminate the opportunities and excuses students have to argue with us, it makes classroom life much easier all round. We can do this by treating them with respect – firmly but fairly – when we give them instructions or deliver consequences. I've outlined some ideas which will help you to phrase instructions without triggering confrontation in 'Six ways to get students to follow instructions' on page 43.

Divide and conquer

This will become something of a recurring theme throughout the book: don't try to deal with the whole group at once. It's easier to get control of a small challenging group than a large challenging group, so split them up and focus on small groups and individuals.

If you set up cooperative learning teams (see page 143), your students will already be in small groups which will help. Build on this, if you need to, by being prepared to separate unruly students from each other, get troublesome individuals working at isolated desks or even ask certain students to join you outside the room for a 'corridor meeting' where you can address their concerns, give warnings and clearly explain consequences without the pressure of an audience. Some kids love to play up in front of their friends and they are much harder to deal with when they are doing so. So put the odds in your favour – divide and conquer!

Keep excellent records

It is imperative that you keep an accurate record when students cause problems in your lessons. Even in the worst of classes there are seldom more than five or six main culprits who are responsible for the bulk of the trouble, so this needn't be as much work as it seems – and the benefits far outweigh the extra work involved.

All you need is an A4 page in your teaching file for each student and in every lesson you record exactly what they say and do to disrupt the class. You then have a vital document which can be used for evidence should you need to speak to parents or senior staff about this child. Being able to quote specific examples such as, 'On 17 March, lesson 2, Jonny called Mark a "fat s***" without provocation and threatened to stab him with a pencil', is far more helpful and professional than a vague complaint like, 'Jonny is always disrupting other students'.

Give the impression of being in control

The way you move and hold yourself in the classroom gives a clear message as to how confident you are feeling. Standing limply with your head on one side, looking at the floor, curling one leg behind the other and clasping your hands are all obvious invitations for a tough class to walk all over you.

In times of stress we all have a range of less obvious gestures and movements which can signify anxiety, such as touching our noses, rubbing our necks or tugging at our clothes. Similarly, when our temper is wearing thin we may clench our fists, tighten our jaw, avoid eye contact or blink rapidly. While quite natural, these actions – which are usually carried out subconsciously – are a clear indication that we are no longer in full control. Young people are experts at noticing when our limits are being reached, and some will take advantage of a teacher they feel is 'losing it'.

Nervous people also tend to move around a lot – shifting their weight from side to side, fidgeting and wringing their hands – so try to keep still. When you're addressing the group, refrain from making lots of wild hand gestures and either plant your feet in one spot or walk very slowly around the room. Aim to take an 'open' posture when you're talking to students – hands at your sides and palms facing upwards – particularly if they are pushing for an argument; it suggests cool, calm confidence.

When moving around the classroom, try to use *all* of the room. This keeps students on their guard, prevents secret plans being hatched in isolated corners and gives a subtle but powerful message that you are in charge. You can make your presence felt at every table quite innocently by checking students' work, offering support and giving praise to individuals or by teaching key points occasionally from the sides and back wall.

And don't forget to smile! If you opt for the 'don't smile until Christmas' routine, you run the risk of turning students against you – and if you're already feeling threatened this will only make things worse. A smile makes you much more approachable and appealing than a frown and it obviously suggests that you're relaxed and comfortable.

Avoid nagging and lecturing

Kids haven't got the time to listen to our lectures – they are just not interested. A deputy head teacher I used to work with seemed to love the sound of his own voice and would take every opportunity to lecture and moan at the kids about their behaviour and why it was unacceptable. Nice as he was, you could see them switch off as soon as he opened his mouth.

We can't win by nagging kids to behave. We have to show them and teach them. We do that by modelling good behaviour ourselves, giving them clear instructions in terms of what to do, offering support and guidance, praising them when they do the right thing and consistently applying consequences when they don't. This takes work but it isn't rocket science.

Establish your support network

There are three main sources of support available to you: your students, your colleagues/management team and parents and guardians.

Gaining support from your students

In my experience the most rebellious, defiant and demanding students can often turn out to be your very best allies in the classroom once you get them on side. This works for two reasons: first, these ringleaders need attention and they will really appreciate the responsibility and, second, they are ringleaders for a reason – other kids follow them and will do as they ask.

Relationships with these students can take time to build but tough ringleaders tend to have an in-built psychological need for attention and recognition. By asking them directly for their assistance, you can give them the acknowledgement and appreciation they crave, while quickly developing a level of mutual trust and respect.

Do this in private – either summon the student(s) in question to your room/ office at breaktime (this will add weight to your request) or catch them in the corridor before the lesson: 'Jonny, the group respond very positively to you, they look up to you. It would be great if we could use your strong personality for the benefit of the class, so how about helping me out by quietening your table down for me? This is what I'd like you to do ...' It's surprising how responsive very challenging students can be when requests are phrased in this way.

Gaining support from colleagues

In terms of support from your fellow staff, the first thing to mention is that the way you enlist their support, particularly in front of a group of students, is extremely important. If you're struggling in the classroom the last thing you want is a colleague marching into your classroom saying, 'I'll take over for you' or 'Just leave this to me'. This can destroy your reputation in a flash, making you look totally incapable.

There are two very effective ways to avoid this while still harnessing the support of your colleagues: coded offers of support and temporary parking.

Coded offers of support

I first came across coded offers of support when I was working at a centre for young people with extreme behaviour problems. Staff were frequently called on to physically restrain students in order to prevent fights and damage to property. On this particular occasion I found myself holding back a teenage boy who had launched a vicious attack on another student in the corridor.

Even though I'd had extensive training in positive handling and restraint procedures (of which, incidentally, I'm not a fan), the struggle quickly became very 'messy'. The more the boy fought, the more determined I became not to let go of him. And the more I tried to reason with him and calm him down, the more aggressive he got. Eventually he was spitting in my face and trying to bite me, and by the time we had migrated to the floor it was painfully obvious that I was making the situation worse.

One by one other members of staff offered to take over from me but I turned them all away – 'I'm fine,' I grunted, dripping with sweat. I didn't want to lose face – my reputation was at stake – and the last thing I wanted was a student thinking I wasn't able to handle him on my own. So we carried on wrestling and our battle soon became something of a spectacle.

Thankfully, and much to my relief, a very experienced colleague arrived at the scene: 'Mr Plevin, there's an urgent call in the office from your wife. She needs to speak to you. Do you want me to take over while you go and answer it?' There wasn't a call from my wife – we both knew that (I wasn't married for one thing) – but the students didn't know that, and this bogus call gave me the opportunity I needed to pull out of the embarrassing stalemate without shame.

My colleague used a coded offer of support which allowed me to stand down without the students thinking I wasn't up to the mark. And with me out of the equation, this angry young man calmed down almost instantly, literally in a matter of seconds. What I learned from this experience is that it's very easy to get ourselves into a deadlock with an angry student, but not so easy for either party to get out of it.

Ordinarily, I believe a teacher should take full responsibility for the management of behaviour in his or her classroom, but when things have got completely out of control a skilled teacher knows when it is time to back down. An irate student doesn't have the emotional control to do this so it is up to us, as adults, to break the standoff. By arranging coded offers of support in advance with your colleagues, you can make provision for such occurrences.

Temporary parking

If you have a very difficult class it's reassuring to have somewhere available to send one or two students during your lesson where they can work under supervision should their behaviour become too disruptive. This is known as 'temporary parking' and is pre-planned with colleagues – perhaps one just down the corridor or in the class next door. In some cases, a student may need to be escorted from your classroom which may require temporary help from an additional member of staff and, out of courtesy, you should always send work to occupy the 'parked' student so that their presence in the temporary classroom isn't too disruptive for your colleague.

One last point concerning support from colleagues – particularly when you are trying to obtain assistance from senior staff or members of the management team – is the importance of keeping comprehensive records with regard to a student's behaviour and the actions you have taken in response to it. Rather than saying, 'I can't handle this group, I need help', it's far better to be able to give specific details. For example, 'This is what I have done … This is what's working with this group … This is what isn't working … This is what they are doing wrong … This is what I can't get them to do … This is what they do when I do this … This is what they do when I do that … Here are some examples …' You will appear far more credible, and are more likely to get the help and support you need, when you are able to give as much detailed background information as possible.

Only park students with a year group either much older or much younger than they are – one in which they will be viewed by the students in the classroom as a nuisance rather than a source of entertainment. Being kicked out of a lesson can be seen as a badge of honour, particularly when the audience is made up of the student's friends.

Gaining support from parents and guardians

Every teacher knows that parental support and involvement can have a huge impact on students in terms of improved attendance, behaviour and achievement, but gaining this support can be problematic. How do we enlist the support of parents and guardians when they seem so unsupportive, uninterested and hard to reach?

First, we must remember they will no doubt have a somewhat negative view of school. They will probably have been summoned to numerous meetings to discuss their child's future and will have a large collection of report cards, detention slips and warning letters cluttering up their sideboard drawers. Focusing on what a student is doing wrong in school is sadly very common and in some cases parents may have had years of constant complaints. Is it any wonder they don't want to get in touch? Indeed, if they themselves failed academically at school (as is often the case), their opinion of the education system in general is not likely to be a favourable one and a call from school is the last thing they'll want to receive.

If you've ever had a bad relationship with your bank then you'll know what I'm talking about: you feel sick every time you get a letter from them reminding you how much trouble you are in. This is often why it is so difficult to win the trust and support of some parents – the last thing they want from school is more bad news.

What we need to do to get these parents on side is to change their negative view of school and their expectation that every communication from a teacher or school representative will be a negative one. Easier said than done? Not necessarily; let's go back to the bank analogy. The way to restore your relationship with the bank when they see you as a huge risk and want nothing to do with you is to give them what they want – positive news about your finances. And it's exactly the same with parents who view school as either irrelevant or threatening – they want positive news about their child.

I know what you're thinking: 'How can I possibly give them good news about Jonny? He never does anything good!' The truth is that *every* child does something to warrant praise from time to time, and we must mark these moments if we want to break the negative cycle. We must look for and acknowledge things to praise and then pass on the good news to parents. And it doesn't matter if it's just a tiny improvement, hardly worthy of mention – the important thing is that we make a *positive* call.

You can probably see how the following 30 second conversation will start to build bonds between school and home:

> Hello, is that Tracy? It's Rob Plevin here from the school. How are you?
>
> It's just a very quick call to let you know that Jonny made a lot of good progress today. I've spoken to his subject teachers and they have all had good things to say about him. Mr Hawkins, his physics teacher, was very impressed and asked me to tell you that he was very pleased to see he had brought his homework in. And I was really happy to hear that he kept himself out of trouble today in geography. He seems to have put last week's silliness behind him.
>
> So that's it really. We're all very pleased – be sure to tell him I called and spoke to you. I'll give you another update in the next few days. Bye.

If you were to repeat this simple process and make two or three of these calls in a week, the parents involved would soon start to change their negative view of the school (and you). But what about the work involved? You haven't got the time to make a call home for each of your students (even if each call only takes up a minute or two of your time)! Well, the good news is you don't have to; initially you just need to concentrate on the students who really need this additional support. That doesn't mean you ignore the good students – they fully deserve that you keep in touch with their parents too. It just means allocating a little extra time where it's needed most, at least initially.

When you make these regular, short, positive contacts with home (either by letter, short note, phone call, text message, semaphore, etc.) parents start to believe, possibly for the first time ever, that someone in authority actually has their interests at heart, and the effect of this cannot be overestimated. Over time, once the telephone conversations start to progress beyond, 'Hello … he was fine today … Goodbye', they may start to see you as a family friend, someone they can trust. And in future they will leap at the chance to offer their assistance. What's more, Jonny will quickly see that school and home are now working together as allies – and that is powerful.

The quick way to build positive relationships with unsupportive parents

With frequent communication you'll find that even the most unsupportive parents soon start to come on side. As this happens, with each subsequent contact, they will share more and more information about the family. Indeed, it is quite common for a caring teacher to be privy to all the latest family news, and this offers a wonderful opportunity to build strong bonds very quickly.

Make a note of the fact that it's grandma's birthday next week or that the man of the house has just got a new job or even that the cat has just had kittens. And then next time you call, make sure you refer back to some of this information, such as asking how grandma enjoyed her birthday, how Mr Brown's new job is going, and can I have a kitten, please? This shows that you listen to them, you care about them and you're not just a nameless face from that school where nobody gives two hoots about them.

Chapter 2
Establishing routines

If you're not already using routines (or 'procedures' to some) in your classroom, then you should be. They can literally transform your classroom overnight, putting your instructions on auto-pilot and making your job much easier.

The first big benefit is saving time – and a lot of it. A great deal of time is lost in the classroom by having to repeat instructions again and again to students who aren't listening. However, once you've taken the time to establish routines the job of getting students to follow your instructions is largely done for you. You no longer have to continually tell them what to do because the routine reminds them exactly what to do and how to do it.

Routines give your students a map to follow and because this map doesn't change, it creates 100% consistency. We all know how important consistency is in terms of teaching and managing behaviour, and routines are really consistency in practice. You simply cannot be inconsistent in the instructions you give to students once you have turned them into a routine.

Routines also give students a greater chance of experiencing success in your lesson – and for our tough, most challenging students, this is something they rarely get to enjoy. By giving them very clear steps to follow in order to complete a given task, the likelihood of them doing the right thing is increased dramatically. And the more opportunities you have to praise students and thank them for behaving appropriately, the more quickly their attitudes and behaviour will change for the better.

Another great thing about routines is that they can be created for almost every transition or behaviour 'hot spot' throughout the school day. For example:

- Entering the classroom.

- The start of the lesson.

- Distributing materials.

- Clearing away materials.

- Asking for help.

- Transitions between activities or tasks.

- What to do when you've finished your task.

- What to do when you're late.

- Using certain equipment.

- Group work.

- Going to the library.

- Watching a video.

- Listening to an outside speaker/visitor.

- Answering questions.

- Handing in class work.

- Handing in homework.

- Leaving the classroom.

How much easier would your teaching day be if you had routines in place for all those difficult times? And how much smoother would the lesson be if students knew exactly what to do in each of those circumstances?

How to set up time saving routines in your classroom

Once you've decided which parts of your lesson would benefit from a routine (usually the more active or less structured periods such as those listed above), setting up routines in your classroom is basically a case of getting your students to follow a numbered checklist – kind of like the one I'm about to give you …

Step 1: Create or write your routine

Writing a routine is essentially a case of boiling down the relevant procedure to a few (three to six) simple steps – just as in the following sample routine for the start of a lesson. (Don't worry if this particular routine seems a little too draconian for your setting – it's just an example.) I've used this exact routine to bring an extremely challenging group of 14-year-olds into line and it worked very well.

1. Arrive on time.

2. Line up in silence.

3. Enter without talking and hang up your coat.

4. Sit in your own seat.

5. Complete the starter activity written on the board.

Step 2: Teach the routine to your class

With very challenging groups there is, of course, an art to giving instructions or introducing a routine successfully. It's a case of walking the 'firm but fair' path and avoiding the shouting, patronising, belittling and threatening while still sticking to your guns and insisting on complete compliance.

For example, to teach the second step in our 'start of the lesson' routine above, you would have the students line up outside the classroom exactly as stated (in silence) and in an orderly manner. If you're happy for them to line up while chatting, pushing and shoving, by all means let them get away with it – but they will do the exact same thing next time you ask them to line up and your routine will fail miserably. It might be better to explain that 'line up in silence' means standing still with your left shoulder touching the wall, hands by your sides, looking straight ahead and saying absolutely nothing.

Pick a handful of students and get them to demonstrate this for the rest of the class to watch, then have the whole class copy them. They will almost certainly test you by getting it wrong – perhaps a little snigger here, a shove there and a total refusal there – so the whole thing has to be repeated.

To make it a bit more fun and less patronising for them, you could try giving them a goal to work to that can easily be reached with practice (e.g. getting everyone lined up in five seconds) and make a game out of reaching the goal. Start slowly, perhaps with a target of 20 seconds on the first day, and speed it up each day from there. Remember to give positive reinforcement along the way.

With some groups you may need to make things a little uncomfortable for them if they don't buy into your instructions when you use the light-hearted game approach. I've known teachers, myself included, spend whole break-times practising 'silent lining up' with a group who preferred to waste time during the lesson when the routine was initially being taught. After a few days of missing their entire break they start to get the message that you mean business.

One more thing: once they have successfully done as you requested it's important to reinforce this. Mark the moment by congratulating them, perhaps with a whole-class spontaneous reward (see Chapter 6 on positive reinforcement).

Step 3: Put the routine on display

The real key to the success of routines lies in making them so well-known to students that they become almost second nature. When something becomes a habit it no longer needs to be taught and when repeating instructions and reminding students is no longer necessary, that is when your classroom becomes truly automated. Once you've taught your routine it needs to be displayed in a prominent place in the classroom as a constant reminder of the relevant steps. And from here on in all you have to do with students who are off task is simply lift a finger and point at the routine displayed on the wall. This then gives you the opportunity to ask one of the most effective, non-confrontational questions for getting students to think about, and take responsibility for, their behaviour: 'What should you be doing right now?' Swiftly followed by: 'Do it then, please.' And as long as you've done a good job teaching that routine they can't really argue with you. Neat, eh?

Make sure you only work on one routine at a time. Early in my training career I was working with a charity to help them improve behaviour at a youth centre. Together we identified the various times and activities throughout the day which would benefit from a structured routine, such as the start of the day, getting on the minibus, minibus behaviour, breaktime – the usual stuff. I knew that routines would make a huge difference to them but the mistake I made was not highlighting the importance of establishing one routine at a time.

The well-meaning and committed staff tried to set up five or six routines at once and it confused the hell out of everyone. I returned a few weeks later to find very little improvement so we went back to basics concentrating on one area at a time.

The difference this made was astounding. The manager called me a few days later to say their working day had been transformed. Lesson learned.

What to do if students won't follow the routines?

One way you can maximise participation in your routines is to involve the students in the creation of them in the first place. Rather than you dictating every aspect of their behaviour – which can seem oppressive, especially for older groups – it can be beneficial to invite the students' suggestions as to how they should act in a particular situation and then use those suggestions to develop the routine. Some groups need steering towards suitable actions, but this can still result in a routine being established much more quickly than when it is simply imposed on them.

I also find that positive peer pressure plays a vital role in a routine being successful, and getting popular members of the group on side is integral to this. Spend a few minutes on a one-to-one basis with some of the ringleaders in the group and explain how important it is to you, and the rest of the group, to have their cooperation. For example:

> Jonny, can I have a quick word? I don't know if you're aware of this but the rest of the class really look up to you and tend to follow what you do. I could really do with using that strong character of yours to help me get the group on side. All I need you to do is help me get this routine established by making sure your group of friends/your table group all follow the steps we agreed. Can you do that? I've asked Kyle and Kieran and they are both keen so you needn't feel you're on your own. Okay?

Despite your best efforts there are always going to be students who feel the need to buck the trend and make it difficult for routines to take root. Often these students need just some individual attention – reminding them that the success of the group depends on everyone taking part in the routine or simply spending a little time trying to find out what is behind their need to ostracise themselves.

Sometimes a firm warning will be enough to get them in line, and if that fails you would naturally move up through your hierarchy of stepped consequences. (I've explained more about the process of delivering consequences in Chapter 4 and on building relationships with students in Chapter 5.)

Be organised and prepared

Having lesson materials, resources and equipment ready in advance can help to maintain routines and avoid those unplanned, unstructured moments during a lesson. Inevitably things go wrong sometimes and you have to rely on your students to be cooperative enough to sit still without messing around noisily while you sort it out. Some groups of students will accommodate temporary hold-ups like this fairly sensibly and patiently but the noisy class won't. To them this is 'cabaret time', and if you don't have activities in place to occupy them, and quickly regain control when they drift, it will soon turn into bedlam.

In reality, many of these situations are completely avoidable. If your most challenging class happens to destroy the classroom while you're busy fiddling with a badly behaved DVD player or doing some last-minute photocopying then you were asking for trouble. Almost all hold-ups, setbacks and glitches can be accommodated by good advance planning.

Here are a few things you could consider:

- Hand-outs and worksheets. It's obvious, I know, but if you have hand-outs to distribute you need sufficient spare copies so you don't need to send someone off to the photocopier mid-lesson.

- Alternative activities. Having back-up resources and alternative activities on standby when something doesn't work out or something goes wrong means you can maintain lesson flow rather than allow students to switch off. You must have something to occupy their attention throughout the entire lesson.

- New activities. If you are trying out new activities for the first time, have a dry run the night before so you can iron out any potential problems. That way, if something does go wrong, you aren't left floundering and can switch immediately to plan B.

- Technical equipment and apparatus. Test everything immediately before the lesson if possible and make sure you have either a technician or spare apparatus on hand. If you're unfamiliar with how to use a piece of equipment, write yourself a simple idiot-proof checklist (Step 1: Plug in the power supply, Step 2: Switch on the power supply, etc.).

- Student equipment. One of the biggest excuses students have for opting out of a lesson activity is the classic 'I haven't got a pen' (or whatever vital piece of equipment is required for the activity at hand). We must pre-empt *all* potential excuses and *all* their possible problems so they don't hold up the lesson. Have a resource box on your desk complete with rulers, pens, pencils, erasers, pencil sharpeners – any and all equipment that might be needed during the lesson. Have it all labelled (with your name on it) so that you can quickly hand a student a ruler, pen or whatsit when they need one without the lesson being disrupted. But don't let them abuse this resource – for more on students who don't bring equipment to class see page 237.

Chapter 3
Giving clear instructions

Issuing clear instructions is about ensuring that we communicate the right message to our students in the right way, so as to minimise confusion and confrontation and to maximise the chances of us getting the behaviour we want.

Much of this comes down to remembering that as much as 75% of communication is non-verbal. It's not so much about the words we use but the way in which those words are interpreted. So it's about body language, facial expressions, hand gestures and our proximity – how close we are to students when we talk to them. All of these have a huge part to play in whether or not other people will really understand what we're saying. Very often students will jump to conclusions or misinterpret what we're saying, and sometimes this happens before we even open our mouths. It's the silent messages we unconsciously give that are often at the root of students' decisions to listen to us, ignore us, shout at us or leave the room in tears.

The way we use our voice also has a large effect on the way our message is interpreted – and in that respect at least, children are very like dogs. (Some are like dogs in many other ways but let's stick with this for now!) If you were to shout aggressively and forcefully at my dog, saying the words: 'I love you, you're such a gorgeous little dog!' he would cower and shrink away fearing he was being berated yet again for nicking one of my shoes. On the other hand, if you were to gently tell him, 'You're a nasty, foul-smelling little hound', in a warm, soothing voice he would lick you enthusiastically and clamber all over you thinking you were his new best friend. He's very fickle. Seriously, though, a dog doesn't understand the actual words used but it does tune into the tone of voice, the pace and the volume. Basically, dogs react to the way we are speaking – as do people.

So, what message are we giving our students through our facial expressions, tone of voice and body language? That we are tired, worn out and close to breaking point? If we do, there is a good chance they will either ignore us or push a little

harder to tip us over the edge when we tell them to do something they would rather not do. Or are we giving them the message that we're angry with them, or that we dislike them? If so, they might well turn against us completely. Tougher students might retaliate there and then, while the more timid ones might hold a grudge and seek retribution at a later date.

We can give the impression that we are a pushover, a threat or a leader depending on the silent messages we communicate, so the way we give instructions will have a massive impact on how students respond to them.

You will find that if you drop the volume of your normal classroom voice to the level you would use to speak in a restaurant, your students may quieten down to listen to you. One of my old teaching colleagues, a very petite woman, had a voice so quiet she was barely audible – the kids in her classroom had to strain to hear her – and her classroom was always very quiet. It was amazing to see how a group behaved in her classroom compared with others where they would be shouting and yelling across the room at each other.

Six ways to get students to follow instructions

1. Give clear instructions in a calm, assertive manner

There are lots of reasons why we should avoid shouting and ranting when we tell students what to do. For one thing, in a class filled with tough, challenging students it virtually guarantees conflict. If we want young people to behave responsibly we need to model what we want to see. Losing your temper and shouting only makes them upset and encourages them to mirror this communication back at you.

For another, they will lose respect for you. Even though some attention deprived children may find some reward in being shouted at (even negative attention is better than no attention at all, right?), it's safe to assume that most kids absolutely hate it. In the short term it may well get them jumping into action, but over time it merely breeds resentment. It also gives some students a sense of power when they witness a teacher who is clearly out of control. For others it provides an entertaining spectacle.

The first aspect of giving clear instructions is to make sure your message can't be misinterpreted. I like to use the analogy of giving students clear tracks to follow when I ask them to do something – in this way there is more chance of them getting where I want them to be, or doing what I want them to be doing, and less chance of an argument. It's simply a case of succinctly explaining to students exactly and specifically what you want them to do.

For example, 'Jonny, you need to stop tapping your pen', 'Stop talking to Kieron' or 'Stop swinging on your chair and look this way', will have more chance of getting the desired outcome than, 'Jonny, stop it!' If Jonny isn't sure what you're asking him to stop doing there is every chance he will argue. 'Stop what? I wasn't doing anything', is likely to be his reply. And if your instructions are going to be crystal clear, we need to avoid vague terms like 'quietly', 'properly', 'sensibly' and 'respectfully' – you know, the ones that are used in every class-room every day. These words have different meanings for different people. What is 'sensible' to us isn't necessarily so to them.

With really obstinate youngsters, vague phrases like, 'Sit properly' and 'Get on with your work quietly please', give them an opportunity for argument. Why? Because we haven't defined *exactly* what we mean by quietly and properly. For one student, quietly means whispering, while for another it means talking in their normal speaking voice. Another student might take this as meaning there is no real rule on noise levels at all. And so when you challenge them, their immediate answer is 'I *am* working quietly!'

If I asked many of my PRU students to 'sit properly', they would argue 'I am sitting properly' – and they would say that while swinging on one single chair leg and doing their best to wear a hole in the carpet. This may sound pedantic but being specific avoids opportunities for 'I am doing as you ask' arguments – and the more arguments we can avoid, the fewer incidents we have to deal with down the line. Wherever there are ambiguous instructions there will be a student breaking the rules. A better instruction than 'sit properly' might be, 'Jonny, sit on your chair like everyone else so that all four chair legs are on the floor. Thanks.'

Similarly, to make sure that students keep within the noise levels we want we need to clarify what we mean by 'quietly'. Younger children might need a tangible representation of the word – for example, they could be shown a ruler and told to use their '30 cm voices' or their 'partner voices' instead of their 'yard voices' (yard being the big concrete thing they play in, not the imperial measurement). For older students, we might simply explain our instruction by demonstrating the volume we want to hear.

And if we want a student to behave 'respectfully', we would do well to explain that this means listening without interrupting, looking at someone when they are talking and being sure to use polite language. This makes it easier for students to do the right thing, which in turn makes it easier for us to manage them.

Finally, what do I mean by a 'calm, assertive manner'? First, use warm, open, non-threatening body language. Frowns and scowls should be replaced by a confident, welcoming smile. There should be no pointing, threatening hand gestures or aggressive posturing. Second, take one slow, deep breath in and out and, as you speak, drop your volume … drop the tone … and slow … the … voice … right … down. This works wonders in getting your message across confidently.

2. Ask the students to confirm that they've heard the instructions

Have you ever asked students to get on with their work only to turn round five minutes later and see that they have totally ignored your instructions? And then when you ask them why they aren't doing as you asked, they say, 'I didn't understand', 'I didn't hear you' or 'I didn't know you were talking to me'.

This is an effective excuse for them because it puts the onus straight back on you. After all, if they haven't understood you, it's your fault. If they didn't hear you, it's your fault. And if they didn't know you were talking to them specifically – your fault again. Your only course of action in this situation (without seeming unjust) is to give them the benefit of the doubt and a second chance. As I said, it's an effective excuse because it legitimately grants them a considerable amount of time off task.

There is a simple solution though. First, get them to confirm or repeat whatever you just asked them to do: 'Jonny, repeat the instructions, please, so I know you heard me.' Following this, you then check that they understood the request: 'Thank you, Jonny. And can you just explain how you would do that so that I know you can do the rest of the questions?'

From there, if Jonny needs additional guidance you give it him but if he indicates he knows how to proceed your job is done. You can then just tell him to get on with it and he no longer has the 'I didn't hear you', 'I didn't know you were talking to me' or 'I didn't understand' excuses.

3. Give them a reason

In 1978, Ellen Langer, a research psychologist investigating human behaviour, was trying to determine the factors which make people more likely to do favours for others.[1] She set up an experiment involving a photocopier machine and tried three different approaches to get people to let them jump the queue:

- Request only: 'Excuse me, do you mind if I go before you to use the photocopier?'

- 'Made up' or irrelevant reason: 'Excuse me, do you mind if I go before you to use the photocopier because I have to make some copies?'

- Real reason: 'Excuse me, do you mind if I go before you to use the photocopier because I'm in a terrible rush?'

So, a third of the time she had people simply ask to skip the queue, a third of the time they gave an irrelevant reason (of course they were there to make copies!) and a third of the time they actually gave a real reason ('I'm in a hurry'). The research yielded interesting results. When the researchers gave a reason for wanting to queue jump they were allowed to do so far more than when simply making the request without a reason. The most surprising part of the study was that it didn't seem to matter what the reason was – a totally irrelevant reason ('Can I go first? I have mice at home') seemed to work just as well as a legitimate one.

The point we can take from this study in relation to our classroom management strategies is that when making a request for a student to do something we should back it up with a reason: 'Can you do this please ... and this is why it would be a good idea ...'

It doesn't necessarily have to be a good reason: 'Get on with your work because otherwise you won't get it finished' should work just as well as, 'Get on with your work otherwise you'll have to spend every lunchtime for the rest of this week working in my office'. And it will undoubtedly stimulate fewer arguments and protests.

---

1   Ellen Langer, Arthur Blank and Benzion Chanowitz, The Mindlessness of Ostensibly Thoughtful Action: The Role of 'Placebic' Information in Interpersonal Interaction, Journal of Personality and Social Psychology 36(6) (1978): 635–642.

Try saying, 'Help me by quietening down please, I have a ~~hangover~~ headache' rather than snapping 'Be quiet!' Or, 'Line up quickly, please, we're running out of time' rather than 'Line up!' Giving the students a reason for doing something also means you can attach importance to the instructions without coming across as officious and bureaucratic. Say, 'When you come to see me at lunchtime, get here for 12.30 p.m. so we can sort this out without it interfering with your lunch too much' rather than, 'See me at lunchtime, without fail!'

Play around with this and see what happens – but don't get carried away or you might get yourself into trouble. 'Give me your dinner money because I'm badly paid' will almost certainly make you unpopular on playground duty.

4. Use closed requests

Starting or ending a request with 'thank you' *before* students have done what you're asking them to gives the clear impression that you expect them to respond positively. We all know the effect of positive expectations so it comes as no surprise that requests phrased in this way tend to give favourable results, often having a quite magical effect on students. Try saying, 'Thank you for lining up straight away' or 'Thank you for doing as I asked – it makes my job so much easier'.

5. Use 'When you do this ... that happens' sentences

In their book, *You Can – You Know You Can*, Maines and Robinson found a 50% reduction in disruptive behaviours following the introduction of a structured script for teachers when giving directions.[2] They suggest that communication can be improved and a situation depersonalised when

2   Barbara Maines and George Robinson, *You Can - You Know You Can: Course Handbook to Accompany Workshops on the Self-Concept Approach* (Bristol: Lucky Duck Publications, 1992).

teachers begin their instructions with, 'When you … (state behaviour)', and end with an explanation of the resulting effect, '… this happens … (state what the behaviour causes)'.

For example, rather than saying, 'You need to stop interrupting' or 'You're holding up the lesson', we would say, 'Jonny, when you shout across the room it disturbs other people. Please get on with your work without shouting.' Or, 'Jonny, when you interrupt me, it makes it difficult for people to hear and I can't teach the lesson properly. Please put your hand up if you want to ask anything.'

6. Use directions instead of questions

We all know we get a better response from students when we treat them with respect rather than hostility, but many teachers – when trying politely to coerce students towards better behaviour choices – make the mistake of asking questions rather than giving direct instructions.

The dialogue tends to go something like this:

> Okay everyone, can we all sit down now?
>
> Jonny, do you think you should be doing that?
>
> Can you get on with your work now, please?
>
> How many more times do I need to tell you?
>
> Would you *please* get on with your work quietly?
>
> Am I talking to myself, Jonny?
>
> Are you ignoring me?
>
> Do you think I'm some kind of idiot?

Not only do questions such as these often result in a reply that you may not want (particularly in the case of the last three), they also convey a lack of real control and therefore often result in arguments. Young people need clear directions not weak questions.

Simple, concise directions delivered calmly and deliberately will work much more effectively than questions if you want students to meet your expectations with minimum fuss: 'Jonny, stop talking. Turn around and finish your diagram now, please.'

Also consider swapping 'please' for 'thank you'. Giving a direct instruction and following it with thank you implies that you expect the student to do as you say: 'Jonny, stop talking. Turn around and finish your diagram, thank you.'

Another way to get students to follow your instructions is to have a stepped hierarchy of consequences in place to back up your request. We will look at consequences in more detail in the next chapter.

Chapter 4
Consequences

Before we get into consequences, I want to hammer home the important message that there are a multitude of effective preventive strategies that we can use to encourage and support students to stay on the right tracks before we need to resort to sanctioning. It's not that I'm against sanctioning; I just feel there is a danger that we can come to rely on consequences (and the threat of them) as the *only* course of action available to us in response to inappropriate behaviour. Managing the classroom in this way can create a very punitive and oppressive atmosphere which usually causes more problems than it solves.

> If you don't do it when I say you'll get a detention.
>
> If I hear one more person shouting you'll all be staying behind at break.
>
> Take that off right now or I'll call your parents.
>
> You haven't done any work all lesson so I'm putting you on report.

Don't get me wrong. We need consequences to enforce boundaries – and kids need boundaries in order to feel secure and learn appropriate behaviour – but like any tool there is a right way and a wrong way to use them.

Correctly applied, consequences can put a near instant end to behaviour infractions at all levels. They can provide a clear, final, definite end point which the student fully understands, while bringing the to and fro of warnings, cautions, threats and other ineffective tactics to a close. Furthermore, they can be a surprisingly effective means to building bonds, particularly with tough, historically defiant students. When a young person senses that his teacher is trying to help him by encouraging and supporting him to make sensible behaviour choices by imposing boundaries firmly yet fairly, his respect, trust and affection for that teacher grows.

One of the biggest benefits to be had from using consequences in the way I explain in this chapter is that they provide the means to manage behaviour at classroom level, rather than clogging up corridors and time-out rooms or running

after-school detentions. Suddenly you have more options available to you when a student does something wrong, and that alone is tremendously empowering.

So let's look at some of the things we can do to make sure we use and apply consequences correctly.

Four ways to make consequences really effective

1. Don't use your big guns straight away – consequences must be stepped

When I first started teaching I didn't have a clue how to control a rowdy class or a student who ignored my instructions. My immediate response was just to repeat the same instructions or threats a bit louder; and when that didn't work I shouted even louder. It's fair to say my skills were limited.

If I was really flustered and caught off guard I would dish out report cards and send students to a senior member of staff (frequently for the most ridiculously minor misdemeanours) in a pathetic attempt to assert my authority. Often the rest of the class would be so surprised and annoyed at my inappropriate responses that they would all join in against me.

Before long I was sending kids out of the room left, right and centre, making threats I didn't have a hope of following through and generally getting myself in an awful mess. The clear message this gives to the students is 'I'm totally incapable of controlling your behaviour so I'm going to send you to someone who can'. If you're looking for a quick way to lose respect in the classroom, this is it.

It soon became clear to me that I couldn't keep sending students out of my class to clog up the senior teacher's office, except in extreme circumstances. These weren't extreme circumstances – it was just an average class of 14-year-old children who wouldn't do their work. Clearly I had a lot to learn.

The turning point came when a more experienced colleague told me that the only way to use consequences effectively was to step them: 'Don't use your big guns straight away, Rob. If you start off by shouting and sending kids out of the room for relatively minor incidents, what are you going to do when the child continues to misbehave? By stepping your consequences you always have the option of adding more if necessary.' Since that day, I can honestly say that my classroom management changed dramatically for the better. It was one of those 'aha' moments when you realise the error of your ways.

Consequences such as loss of break, being kept back after school or before lunch are great because you can start off with quite small increments of time to get your point across and then keep adding to them. You don't have to take a child's whole breaktime away if they are chatting in your lesson, and you certainly don't need to jump straight to the (largely ineffective) threat of an after-school detention. Start by taking two minutes and if that has no effect you can move up from there.

Even a two minute delay can be an incredibly effective consequence because young people always have somewhere else they would rather be, particularly when their friends have already left. It may not sound like much of a sanction, but at the end of the lesson, when their friends are all leaving to go to lunch and they have to stay behind to explain themselves to you, even a minute can seem like an eternity. To make consequences fair it's about the certainty – the fact that *something* happens – rather than the severity.

In the following example you'll see that by starting small we have multiple options to step the consequence and continue to address the student's behaviour should it continue.

Step 1: Jonny, you can stop talking and go to break with everyone else after the lesson, or you can carry on talking and I'll keep you behind for two minutes at breaktime. It's your choice.

Step 2: Okay, Jonny, you've already lost the first two minutes of your break. If you don't want to lose your whole breaktime you need to pick up the eraser you just threw on the floor.

Step 3: Jonny, that's your whole break gone, I warned you. Now, unless you want me to keep you behind after school I suggest you settle down and get the work finished.

Beyond this, of course, you do need to be prepared for students who continue to ignore you. With a noisy class you are likely to encounter students who may even need to be removed from the class at times, so this response should feature in your hierarchy of consequences. And you should, ideally, have a 'stock hierarchy' in mind, or even written down, which you can use in response to general incidents of inappropriate behaviour.

Here's an example of a hierarchy of stepped consequences similar to one I used to use in my classroom:

A. **Warning**

'Jonny, your talking is distracting everyone. You don't need to discuss anything right now so work in silence please. If you carry on talking you will have to move to the chair at the front and work on your own.'

The warning phase can be adapted to almost any situation with the exception of behaviours which require an immediate consequence such as acts of violence, vandalism, verbal abuse and so on.

B. **Move to isolated seat at front of classroom for a set amount of time (e.g. ten minutes)**

'Jonny, you have made the choice to sit on your own next to my desk. I'll set a timer for ten minutes and if you can sit quietly and get on with your work I'll let you go back to your normal seat. If you continue to mess around, you can stay there for the rest of the lesson.'

C. **Removal from the classroom**

'Jonny, it's clear you're not going to listen to me today so it's best that you go next door and work in Mr Smith's class. Pack up your things. Any work you don't get finished will need to be completed at break.'

(See 'temporary parking' on page 28 for more information on having students removed from the classroom.)

D. **Two minute follow-up**

Although I've put this as step 4, the two minute follow-up can fit pretty much anywhere in your consequence hierarchy and, arguably, can be employed in response to most misdemeanours occurring during a lesson. A student who habitually forgets their equipment, is constantly out of their seat, purposefully disrupts other students or continually avoids work tasks, for example, will benefit from more than a brief reprimand or warning when the offending behaviour is displayed. The two minute follow-up provides an opportunity to discuss the issue and to attempt to find longer term solutions.

It also provides a means to follow up on issues which would otherwise disrupt the flow of the lesson were they to be addressed as they occur. For example, if a student is 15 minutes late to class, the best time to have them explain their reasons isn't when they walk through the door as it will likely unsettle the other students. Better to direct them to sit down, give them brief directions about the task they should be working on and then speak with them at the end of the lesson about their punctuality. (For more ideas on dealing with poor punctuality see page 240.)

E. **Ten minute detention**

I would rank the ten minute detention as your top tier sanction for use at classroom level (i.e. without necessitating involvement from other parties) because it is incredibly effective when done right. Beyond this you are into full after-school detentions, report cards, letters/phone calls home and other such sanctions as listed in your school behaviour policy. And the reason I feel it to be so effective is precisely down to that fact. When you manage discipline at a classroom level you naturally gain a certain level of respect from your students – they see *you* as the one in control.

There is a full explanation of the two minute follow-up on page 61 and the ten minute detention on page 64.

Rather than moving mechanically through the levels of your hierarchy (I've seen teachers do this intentionally, and rapidly, so that a problematic student gets removed from the class as soon as possible), be prepared to offer some level of additional support along the way.

Often the behaviour we witness in the classroom is a cry for attention or help, and we need to be sensitive to students who may be struggling with a whole range of emotional, social and educational issues. A 'problem child' is always 'a child with a problem', one who will certainly benefit more from some patience and understanding than a succession of cold, dispassionate threats and warnings. The hierarchy of consequences is necessary – it gives us, and our students, the all-important boundaries – but it is far better to help students work within those boundaries rather than to let them go crashing through them.

This might mean allowing a student a little space outside the classroom for a while ('Go and have a little walk down the corridor, Jonny, to get your thoughts together - be back in here by quarter past'), providing additional learning support ('Let's team you up with Ringo for a while to help you on these questions') or just showing that you care about them by being a little more compassionate in the way you speak to them ('I know you're finding things tough right now. Let's take the pressure off because I don't want you having to be sent out if we can help it. Come and sit here and have ten minutes on your own sitting quietly. If you need to talk to me, or if you feel yourself getting wound up again, just raise your hand and you can let me know what's on your mind in private').

2. Keep your cool – consequences must be delivered calmly

If you lose your temper when you give warnings and consequences, you pass control to your students. Leaders don't lose control, they remain ice cool. They don't shout and scream because they know people will lose faith in them. If you want to have control in the classroom, you must be that unruffled, cool, calm leader.

Surprisingly, consequences are actually the perfect tool to help you remain composed in the face of misbehaving students. How? By letting the consequence do the job of controlling behaviour. There is no need for you to lose your temper when you issue a consequence. Just calmly state what will happen if the behaviour continues and then walk away, job done. Simply give the warning safe in the knowledge that if the student doesn't do as you asked, the consequence will kick in. That way you can remain calm and collected while the threat of the consequence does its work.

 When you give warnings and issue consequences to individual students, do so quietly so that other students can't hear. It makes it less embarrassing for the student in question and less entertaining for the rest of the class.

3. Firm but fair – the consequence must fit the crime

When we're faced with the huge variety of behaviour issues which any noisy class presents, it's easy to slip into a one-size-fits-all approach in terms of the consequences we use. An after-school detention (or threat of) is the usual stock response to any and all misdemeanours, but as a deterrent or solution detentions are pretty useless. While it's true that the threat of a detention can quickly get a normally quiet, well-behaved child into line, it has little effect on strong willed, non-compliant children. It might work with those who already behave but it won't work on those who need to learn to behave – other than making them even more angry and resentful. And with most detention activities falling into the 'You've wasted my time so I'll waste some of yours' category, the time spent by students in detention is more often than not completely pointless.

With a little thought, however, consequences can be more closely linked to the behaviour in question. And by structuring warnings carefully and offering clear choices we can encourage students to take more responsibility and become more accountable for their behaviour without the usual hostility associated with detentions and punishments.

In case you are wondering how to come up with suitable consequences for the many behaviour problems you encounter on a daily basis, I've got a formula which works quite well in most circumstances:

suitable consequence = behaviour problem + restricted access

In other words, a suitable consequence generally involves temporary removal or limited access to whatever was causing the problem. For example:

- Misuse of equipment: restrict access for a short while. 'You know you're not supposed to wear headphones. Put your headphones away or you'll have to put them in my locker until the end of the lesson.'

- Wasting time: take away some of their time. 'Jonny, you've wasted ten minutes of lesson time. If you can't get the work caught up in the remainder of the lesson, you'll have to return at the start of breaktime to catch up.'

- Disrupting the lesson: separate them from the activity/their peers temporarily. 'You've shown me that you can't work sensibly as part of your group. You can sit next to me and work on your own for the next ten minutes. If you manage to do that I'll let you return to the group. I'll set a timer.'

4. Be consistent – consequences must always be followed through

We all know consistency is essential in teaching but in terms of delivering consequences it is particularly crucial. Issuing threats you can't carry through is the quickest way to ruin your reputation in school and wreck your chances of controlling difficult groups. If a student gets away with something once they will expect to get away with it again, and if you threaten a consequence and then back down on it you very clearly give the message that your rules are like the weather – changeable. Very soon you will become known as a push-over, a teacher who has no chance of commanding respect or getting students to do as they are asked, and you will have very effectively trained them not to follow your instructions. If you give a warning, the consequence must follow every time.

How to make consequences work like magic

Here's a useful little phrase to add every time you give a warning to a student: 'Is that what you want to happen? It's your choice'. It really gets them thinking about their behaviour and helps them to make sensible choices. So, when added to a warning for an impending consequence, it would look something like this: 'If you don't manage to get the work that I've set for you finished, you will end up losing five minutes of breaktime. Is that what you want to happen? It's your choice'.

By adding this simple little phrase you'll be amazed how much more effective warnings become. I suppose it comes down to the fact you're doing two very important things here: helping them really think about where their behaviour is leading them ('Is that what you want to happen?') and then reminding them that the way out is completely within their control – that they have a clear choice ('It's your choice').

The two minute follow-up

The two minute follow-up is a consequence you can use in response to students who have caused a fairly minor problem during your lesson – those who have forgotten to bring equipment, who were late to the lesson, who are making silly comments in class or who are not completing work when asked. It takes place immediately after your lesson, as soon as other students have been directed to leave.

If your lesson happens to fall just before breaktime or lunchtime, and if you've found the student's behaviour particularly tiresome, you might be tempted to make the two minutes drag on and become four or five minutes. But you should keep this particular consequence to no more than two minutes.

What we're aiming for here is for students to see that you are fair and approachable, but that you also consistently follow up on any and all misdemeanours. We want to let them know that their behaviour was unacceptable and then encourage them to make necessary changes going forward. If you spend their whole breaktime lecturing them, they will lose respect for you and change is unlikely.

Here are four key points to get across to students during a two minute follow-up.

1. Set the tone for the meeting and state what they did wrong

This is not a time to rant and rave at students. They are likely to be feeling annoyed at not being able to leave with their friends, and perhaps a little apprehensive at the prospect of being told off, so we need to show that this is more about finding solutions rather than dwelling on mistakes. Reassure them that this is just going to be a very quick follow-up and that the purpose is to help prevent them getting into further difficulty or trouble.

Example 1: 'Okay Jonny, the reason for this meeting is that you were ten minutes late today and this isn't the first time I've had to tell you about this. Agreed? I don't want to be on your case all the time, so we're just going to quickly look at some ways we can stop this happening in the future ...'

Example 2: 'Jonny, we seem to be clashing quite a lot recently and I'm having to give you too many warnings about your rudeness and bad language. I want you to have a chance at succeeding here, so shall we try to work out some ways we can work well together without these recurring problems?'

2. Briefly explain why their behaviour is a problem

Refer to school policy, their own learning/future and/or the effect on other people: 'When you're late it means my lesson is disrupted and that's a problem for your classmates as well as me. It also means you have to catch up work in your own time.'

In some cases you might consider showing them what they were doing by role playing or acting out what they did so they can get a clearer picture of why this is a problem during the lesson: 'Do you mind if I show you what I saw you do?' or 'This is what I saw when you "brushed past" Jake.'

Note: Avoid this form of role play with students who are on the autistic spectrum and be wary of doing this with students who are likely to respond aggressively when confronted in this way.

3. Get their side of the story and give them opportunity to suggest a solution

When establishing the student's reasons for their behaviour, avoid asking them why they did it – for example: 'Why do you have to behave like this?'

'Why won't you listen?' 'Why are you always late?' 'Why don't you ever bring your homework?'

Starting a question with 'why' is incredibly confrontational. If you don't believe me, just try bombarding your spouse/partner/children with questions like, 'Why isn't dinner ready?' 'Why is your room untidy?' 'Why haven't you taken the dog out yet?' for the first few minutes when you get home tonight and see what sort of reaction you get.

Instead of asking why, ask students *how* they think they might stop the behaviour from happening again, *what* would need to happen in order to prevent it happening again and *who* they might seek help from if they need it.

4. Create a one-step plan for improvement

Work together to come up with one key action the student could take to reduce the chance of the problem happening in the future and tell the student to focus on this for the next week. Set up a brief review meeting with the student for a week from now if you feel it necessary and be sure to congratulate him/her on progress made as the week progresses.

Note: If a student absconds at the end of the lesson and fails to attend your two minute follow-up, never chase after them; the likelihood of you looking olish is quite high. Instead, remain calm and later in the day send a message via their form teacher that they are to attend a ten minute detention with you after school. For obvious reasons, in these litigious times, always leave the door open when you are having a one-to-one conversation with a student.

The ten minute detention

In most schools teachers have the authority to keep a student for five or ten minutes after school without needing to contact parents. The key is that when they do so they give the clear message that they are fully in control of incidents in their classroom and are fully prepared to deal with them personally, without needing to pass the buck and involve other staff, such as senior teachers or those monitoring after-school group detentions.

It's interesting that while some would see ten minutes as an inconsequential amount of time, there are several advantages. Just five or ten minutes is enough to be inconvenient for the student without being seen as unfair, so the ten minute detention doesn't provoke resentment like normal detentions do. Also, it's a lot easier to get a student to show up for a ten minute detention than a one hour detention which they see as a total waste of time.

As with the two minute follow-up, this isn't a time to lecture them or rant at them; rather it's a time for them to suggest ways in which they can avoid a repeat performance of their behaviour so as to progress and succeed. It's ironic that even though both the two minute follow-up and the ten minute detention are both consequences or sanctions, implementing them often strengthens relationships between teacher and student. This is because the teacher works with the student in a supportive rather than punitive fashion; and students grow to respect a member of staff who is willing to give up their time to help them.

The conversation in the ten minute detention will follow roughly the same pattern as the two minute follow-up, but the additional time gives greater opportunity for the student to express his/her feelings and to discuss solutions in more detail. Providing the student with a reflection sheet gives them the opportunity to give their side of the story (without feeling they are being interrogated) and also gets them thinking about what they could do differently in future in a similar situation.

You can download a copy of the reflection sheet from: www. noisyclass.com/bookresources.

What if they don't show up?

Most students will show up. As your reputation spreads as a fair, consistent teacher who is there to help them succeed, you will find that their respect for you grows exponentially. But for the stubborn few who flaunt every rule in the book you have to move up to the next gear. You have two choices as to how you do so.

The first is to initiate the school behaviour system and issue the relevant consequence/sanction. This way you give the clear message that there are no second chances, that your decision is final and that you will not be messed around.

The second involves more work, and while some would argue that you are giving students an extra warning, my reasoning is that you are showing you will do your utmost to make sure students follow your rules and manage their behaviour without involving others. In my experience this is by far the best method for building bonds with tough students and for gaining their respect in your classroom. In terms of the work involved, don't be put off. The extra few minutes spent doing this will pay massive dividends in future in terms of your relationship with, and your ability to manage, the student in question. And that's going to save you a lot of time in the long term.

For this method you need to track the student down – at breaktime, lunchtime or during registration – and explain to them that they must do the ten minutes some time during the next 24 hours. It doesn't really matter when – breaktime, lunchtime or after school – but they need to give you ten minutes of their time.

The following note (or similar) can be given to the student with the instruction to pass it on to his parent/guardian:

> Dear Mrs Smith,
>
> I'm trying to address the fact that Jonny is missing a considerable amount of work through being late for most of my lessons. To help him catch up, and to discuss ways that I can help him, I asked him to stay behind yesterday for ten minutes after school, but he failed to show up. I don't want to escalate the matter and make it an issue for the school to sort out at this stage, so I would appreciate it if you could let him know that he has one last chance to give me ten minutes of his time – either before school starts, during break/lunch or after school tomorrow ...

You should also mention to the student that you will be telephoning home later that day to check that it has been received. This gives them an obvious opportunity (and you can spell it out to them if you need to) to do the ten minutes without their parent needing to see the note. Sneaky, I know, but it works wonders.

 ## Four steps for delivering consequences effectively

This four step script can be used as a framework for delivering consequences without fights and fuss in response to most forms of disruption in lessons.

1. Give a clear warning

State very clearly what the student is doing wrong and what they have to do to put it right. Remember not to get angry or raise your voice – you don't want to reward their behaviour with an emotional outburst and you don't want to antagonise them. Let the consequence do the job for you as you calmly state what will happen if they continue: 'Jonny, you're not doing your work. You need to pick up your pen and finish your target so that you don't have to get it finished in your own time,' or 'If you don't manage to finish the work, you are going to lose five minutes of your break catching up,' or 'If you don't stop throwing bits of eraser, you'll have to spend your break clearing the entire floor.'

At this stage, once a warning has been given, students often start to complain. Don't get drawn in by this and don't discuss the matter further. If you engage with them at this stage they will think there is a chance that you will change your mind – and once they see an opening they will try to exploit it with more and more arguing. A brisk, 'I've told you what your choices are,' is all you need to say and then walk away.

2. Give them 'think time' to process your instruction/warning

Once a clear warning has been given it is important to give the student some time to process what you've said. The reason we do this is because it is very difficult for a student to back down in front of their peers, particularly if you are standing over them waiting for them to comply.

By backing off – walking to another part of the room or going to help another student – you take pressure off them so there is more chance of them doing the right thing: 'Jonny, I'm going to help Kieron for a minute so you can think about what choice you're going to make while I do so. When I come back to your desk in one minute from now I need to see that you've made a start.'

When you explain clearly and exactly what they are doing wrong, what the consequences will be and what they must do to put it right, it's surprising how quickly they will change their behaviour. You are still maintaining total control and managing the situation but in a manner they will see as fair.

How much more sensible is this than losing your temper, giving them lots of negative attention and confusing them with idle threats that you won't follow up? Or worse, really losing your temper and looking a twerp in front of the rest of the class?

But we're not finished yet. We want to acknowledge this behaviour change so there is more chance of it being repeated in future.

3. If they do as you ask, acknowledge it

Assuming that Jonny has heeded your warning and is now back at work, you need to acknowledge that – this is a big step he's just taken. Don't fall into the trap of lecturing him about how he should follow instructions faster next time. Just give him a sincere smile and whisper some quiet one-to-one praise: 'I'm impressed Jonny – well done. Thank you for doing as you were asked, it makes my job much easier!' Younger students can be rewarded more formally, perhaps by getting them to place a sticker on a chart for meeting a relevant behaviour target such as 'Follow teacher's instructions'.

4. If they don't do as you ask, issue your first consequence

If the student doesn't do as you've asked, this is the time to move on to your first consequence – and state it calmly, without emotion: 'Okay you've chosen to carry on doing (insert behaviour). That's fine. You'll be staying in at break for five minutes. Now get on with your work so that you don't lose any more of your time.'

Once again, give them a few moments to think and settle. If the student continues to ignore you after this, or if the behaviour resumes after a few minutes of respite, repeat steps 1 to 4 with the next consequence in your hierarchy. This is why it is crucial to have a stepped range of consequences ready to use so that you can increase the severity without losing control.

How to avoid getting drawn into secondary behaviours and backchat

Whenever you have to issue a consequence to a student you will almost certainly provoke some eye rolling, muttering, complaining and other secondary behaviours. Don't get drawn into these attempts to start an argument; it will escalate until either the student does something that will cause you more stress or you will explode and embarrass yourself. Either way you can't win by arguing.

To prevent this, remember that the easiest way to prevent a fight is simply to deny the other person anyone to fight with. So, when you hear comments like, 'It wasn't me! Everyone else was talking! Why are you picking on me?' you might find the following stock responses very useful:

> You made your choice. Case closed.

> If you want to talk more about this we can do it later. Come and see me after school – I'll be in my room.

> I don't want to argue with you about this because it's going to make us both look foolish and it's going to stop everyone else from learning. If you want to talk more about it come and see me after the lesson; for now, get on with your work.

> I can only deal with what I see, just like a football referee. Sorry, case closed.

As soon as you've given your response, walk away. Busy yourself with another student or some other task so that it's clear you're not going to enter into any more discussion.

The amazing three requests technique for delivering consequences

This is a really effective way to keep your cool when dealing with the most demanding students in the most frustrating, anxiety filled situations. I have witnessed this technique, almost overnight, play a major role in turning a student referral unit where I was working – where the extremely damaged and challenging young people ran wild (and where the committed but powerless staff were in tears) – to a centre of excellence where students came to lessons with smiles on their faces and enjoyed the opportunity to achieve. Needless to say, the staff enjoyed the changes too.

Having used this strategy in several settings over many years since then, I have found it to be a very effective method for gaining compliance from very disobedient and challenging students who display extreme and entrenched behaviour problems.

The main benefits of the three requests technique include:

- The member of staff has a very simple script to follow which promotes total consistency – both on a personal level and between other members of staff.

- The script means staff members always have a response they can calmly rely on, even when under immense pressure. They don't need to try to think of something to say on the spot – they just use the script.

- It eliminates the need to shout, lose your temper and repeat instructions over and over again.

- It prevents the issuing of sanctions and punishments which the students would consider unfair and which could therefore lead to further confrontation.

- It gives students an opportunity to address their behaviour and make appropriate choices.

- It leads to a known, prearranged consequence (e.g. time out, phone call home, ten minute detention), so it can be used with any pre-existing behaviour policy or hierarchy of consequences.

The best way of explaining the process is by way of an example. Let's consider the following response to a student (our old friend Jonny) who keeps getting out of his chair and walking round the room.

The teacher, on recognising that Jonny is agitated about something, first tries the many preventive strategies she has at her disposal: she tries offering more support (she asks him if anything is wrong or offers him more help with his work), she gives him a work target, she offers him limited choices (e.g. an alternative seat), she praises other students in the room and so on.

But Jonny continues to get out of his chair, walk around the room and bother other students. Clearly it's time for phase one of the three requests technique. The teacher says (in a very calm tone): 'Jonny, you're out of your chair. Please return to your seat and get on with your work.' The teacher then turns away for a few moments to look at another student's work and to give Jonny time to follow her request without losing face in front of his friends.

Jonny continues to walk round the room. At this point the teacher moves closer to him and repeats her instruction in a calm, non-confrontational manner: 'Jonny, I'm asking you for the second time to return to your seat.' At this stage it is crucial to maintain a calm voice – the teacher doesn't need to raise her voice or get angry – she just lets the script do the work.

If Jonny complied at this point the teacher would reinforce the fact that he had followed instructions by immediately giving him some praise to reward his behaviour. She wouldn't berate or lecture him for not following her initial instructions and she wouldn't ignore the fact that he had managed to take a very positive step by changing his behaviour.

However, if Jonny didn't do as he was asked at this stage then the teacher would ensure she had his attention and the instructions would be repeated one last time: 'Jonny, this is the third and final time I'm going to ask you to sit down and get on with your work.' It's important that the instruction is brief and direct, but again, the voice isn't raised or accompanied by an emotional reaction of any sort. She doesn't get drawn into debates, arguments or explanations. Jonny knows exactly what he has to do to avoid a consequence; there is no need to provide any further reasoning.

If Jonny finally managed to follow the request he would be praised as above. If he still persisted in behaving inappropriately he would then be notified of the consequence: 'Jonny you were asked three times to sit down. You haven't done as I said. You must (insert prearranged consequence).'

Here are some examples:

> Jonny, you were asked three times to sit down. You haven't done as I said. Go to time out.

> Jonny, you haven't followed instructions. Pack up your things and come and sit at one of the single desks at the front. Thank you.

After issuing the consequence, the teacher would then look out for any demonstration of positive behaviour by Jonny which she can then praise. The approach must be to give attention to the right behaviour whenever possible and to apply the consequence in a calm, non-emotional way.

When using the three requests technique, it is important to bear in mind the following points:

- Don't use the technique for secondary behaviours. If it is over-used it will cause more problems than it solves. By secondary behaviours I mean smirks, comments made under the breath, the sighs and rolling eyes from students in response to a consequence you've just given them. Ignore them, don't get drawn into an argument and certainly don't start going through the script again.

- The technique is best used with *one* consequence every time – and preferably one which can be applied *immediately* such as moving to an isolated chair in the classroom, time out, withdrawal from an activity or similar. Once students know that the warnings *always* lead to the same outcome, the technique becomes extremely effective.

- Don't rush through the three stages. I've seen teachers scream: 'First time, second time, third time … time out!' and this is clearly wrong as it gives the student no time to process each request. Don't get angry if they ignore you the first time or even the second time. That's the beauty of this technique – you don't need to. Just let the script and the known consequence do the work for you.

- You don't have to use three warnings – in other parts of this book I have mentioned the need for just one warning when giving consequences. Don't get too caught up in the details at this point, and by all means adapt the script to suit your particular style or setting. I wouldn't advocate giving more than three warnings in any circumstances, but there is certainly an argument for adjusting the script to accommodate just one or two. The important thing is that your students are clear as to how many warnings there are and that you are consistent in applying them.

How consequences can put an immediate end to behaviour problems

Before we end this chapter, let's look at consequences in action and see how effective they can be to stem behaviour problems – when used correctly.

Below are three very different possible scenarios involving a challenging teenager who is wearing headphones in class. In the first, the teacher is led on a lengthy and stressful battle of wills in which the student does everything possible to avoid following instructions. In the second, the teacher is quick to respond, although does so with something of a hostile/punitive approach. This leads to further arguments and results in the student storming out of the room. In the third example, we see how fair consequences, calmly and consistently applied, eliminate much of the time, frustration and stress of trying to manage behaviour.

Example 1

The student comes into the class wearing headphones. The teacher ignores the behaviour because of a fear of repercussions from challenging this aggressive student. The student parades around the room, clearly aware of the teacher's reluctance to challenge him. The teacher continues to ignore the behaviour but gets increasingly annoyed and frustrated. The student sits with his back to the board nodding to the music.

> Teacher: Can you put your headphones away, please? If you don't you know I'll have to take them off you.
>
> Student (sneering): Aye, yer can try.

The student ignores the warning and carries on listening to music and laughing with his friends. The teacher avoids the issue and goes to speak to other students. Eventually, the teacher reluctantly gives another warning, knowing that the student is in control.

> Teacher: Look, I'm asking nicely. Please take your headphones out and put them away or give them to me.
>
> Student: Yer can't take them off me, they're mine.

The teacher explains that headphones are against the school rules.

> Student: Yeah, but I'm not doing any harm – I can still hear you.
>
> Teacher (becoming more frustrated): That's not the point – it's against the rules.

The student continues to ignore the teacher, so the teacher changes tack and tries to cajole and reason with the student.

> Student: I'll turn the music off then and just leave the headphones in.

The teacher repeats the instructions using more cajoling and reasoning – until they eventually explode or leave the room in tears.

Example 2

The student comes into the class wearing headphones.

> Teacher: Get those out of your ears and in your pocket!

The student mutters something unsavoury and slowly takes the headphones out, leaving them dangling around his neck.

> Teacher: What did you say to me?
>
> Student: Nothin'.
>
> Teacher: It better had have been nothing. You come in here thinking you can do whatever you want. It's not happening in my classroom. Put the headphones away. NOW!
>
> Student: God! Keep your hair on, stress head!
>
> Teacher (throwing the door open and pointing to the corridor): Out!

The student grabs some textbooks off a desk, flings them to the floor and stomps out of the room.

Example 3

The student comes into the class wearing headphones. The teacher notices the headphones straight away but greets the student warmly, before calmly giving a warning.

> Teacher: Hi Jonny. How are you doing today? Did you manage to get to the match at the weekend? Good result, eh? Now, what's our rule on headphones in lessons? Put them away because otherwise I'll be in trouble for not sticking to school rules … Thanks Jonny. If I see them out again I'll have to confiscate them, okay?

Jonny takes the headphones out, but five minutes later the teacher notices he's wearing them again.

> Teacher: Jonny, I warned you about the headphones. Give them to me, please. I don't want to keep them but I do want to save you from getting into

> more trouble and having to hand them in to the office. I'll put them in my desk drawer so that nobody else can touch them, and you can have them back at the end of the lesson.

Some students will hand over the headphones at this early stage – if they know you are consistent in following up and applying further consequences and if they have found you to be fair in the past. However, some students will try to push further.

> Student: It's okay. I'll just put them in my pocket.

The teacher moves closer so as to speak to Jonny quietly out of earshot of other students, or asks Jonny to join him in the corridor so they can talk without an audience which will make it easier for Jonny to stand down without added peer pressure.

> Teacher: Jonny, I don't want your headphones and I don't want you to lose them. Let's not let this get out of hand. I've got this bag – the headphones can go straight in there without me even touching them. I'll put them in my drawer and you can come and get them out of the drawer at the end of the lesson … (pauses to give Jonny time to respond) You can either hand them to me now and you'll get them back at the end of the lesson, or if this goes on any longer I'll take them to the school office and your parents will have to come in and collect them, which means you'll be without them for a while. I don't want that and neither do you, so come on, put them in the bag. It's your choice.

In the third example you can see how the teacher is fully in control throughout the incident. At each stage, there is always a consequence in hand and there is no need to get frustrated or angry.

Chapter 5

The number one secret to effective classroom management

After 25 years of working with emotionally damaged and 'difficult' children, I've come to the conclusion that there is just one true key to successful behaviour management. It really doesn't matter how many 'proven' strategies you have in your arsenal because without this, your efforts will almost certainly come unstuck. The secret ingredient, sadly overlooked by many teachers particularly those of the punishment-focused, oppressive variety is … (drumroll please) a positive teacher–student relationship.

I once read the story of a teacher who returned to teaching after a career break and found himself struggling to manage the behaviour of his students. He was laughed at and ignored by the students and many of his lessons were completely out of control. This same teacher happened to have co-authored a highly respected book on classroom management, he was a qualified psychologist, a senior teacher with more than 15 years' classroom experience and later became a university lecturer in teacher training. This presents something of a conundrum. Here we have a very experienced and intelligent teacher who finds himself totally unable to control his students, despite having written a comprehensive textbook on dealing with classroom behaviour problems. He knows all the theories, he's got all the skills and strategies and yet he can't get the kids to behave. What's going on? How can this be?

Well, the answer is that he had no relationship with his new cohort of students – he didn't know them and they didn't know him. And because they didn't know him, they could neither trust him nor respect him. How can you really trust someone you don't know?

This teacher had returned to the classroom thinking that all the wonderful theories, strategies and case studies he had carefully explained in his book would help him swiftly brush aside any of the classroom problems he was likely to encounter. But he had forgotten one of the most important principles of successful teaching: students will always respond more positively to a teacher they know, like and trust; they will always work harder and behave better for a teacher they get on with. (I should add that this teacher was quick to realise his error and promptly set about resolving his predicament. He began focusing heavily on his relationship with the students and saw an almost immediate improvement in their attitudes and behaviour.)

It can be easy to blame the system – the school, the setting, the building, the students, the parents, the lack of support from senior staff, the policies – for disorder in the classroom, but these factors have no real relevance for the teacher who has a good relationship with his or her students. Teachers with relationships at the core of their practice are able to go into virtually any classroom, in any school, and succeed with even the most difficult of students.

In this chapter I'm going to show you some of the best, fast acting ideas and strategies I know of for building positive relationships with hard to reach students and becoming the teacher they respect and value. You really *can* get them to respond more constructively to your instructions and you really *can* see miraculous transformations in terms of their attitudes towards you when you make positive relationships a priority.

Why bother with all this relationship building stuff?

Some teachers tell me they haven't got the time for this – their job is to teach students, not like them. They teach 300 students a week and could never get to know them all anyway. They have too much paperwork to do and so on. I sympathise – I've been there too. I know how much pressure teachers are under. So my best answer to the 'Why bother?' question is that doing this is actually going to *save* you time in the long run, and it will make your job much easier and far more enjoyable.

A few years ago I was talking with a friend of mine after delivering training at his school. He (let's call him John) told me a story about one of the teachers at the school (she can be called Janet for the purpose of this story and for the benefit of any Terry Wogan fans) who was struggling badly with one particular group of students. She just couldn't get them quiet.

John was Janet's head of department and he often had to pass through her room when she was teaching in order to get resources from the main store cupboard. He told me that on one particular day he happened to be passing through when Janet was teaching her most challenging group.

The students were literally out of control – screaming, shouting and totally ignoring Janet's cries to settle down. John didn't normally intervene unless asked to do so but he felt this situation was only going to get worse, so he walked around the room speaking quietly to some of the students for a few minutes. Without the need to raise his voice, a hush gradually descended on the room and the students returned to their seats facing Janet – happy faces, ready to work.

John quietly left the room and went about the rest of his day without giving the incident a second thought. At the end of the school day, when the students had left the premises, Janet caught up with John in the staffroom. 'John, how do you do that? How the hell do you manage to get that group so quiet so easily?' she asked. 'They won't do anything I say and yet they settle straight away for you. I spend the whole lesson fighting with them. What do you do? What is it? What's the secret?'

I'm sure she didn't expect the reply he gave her. She wanted a magic bullet, a sure-fire strategy, a new way of giving instructions, a secret hand signal or a never-fail script to follow. But I hope she understood the power of what he said and I hope you do too – it's priceless. It is the single, most important tool any teacher can develop and it leads to an enviable level of respect from your most challenging students.

'There's no magic to it,' he said. 'It just boils down to this: I *know* these kids. I've spent time with them. I go to support them playing football for the school at weekends, I chat with them in the corridor, I regularly speak to their parents on the telephone, I visit their homes, I've taken them on trips and I sit with them at lunchtime. The door to my room is always open to them – they know they can come and chat when something's wrong – and I make a point of catching up with them whenever I can.'

I maintain, as my friend does, that there is no 'magic' to successful classroom management other than making positive relationships the foundation of your overall approach. With that said, here are some strategies to help.

The two essential factors for building positive relationships fast

We know how important positive teacher–student relationships are and that they are at the heart of good teaching. But the big question is this: how do we go about building them? I mean, specifically, what are the *exact* steps that we should take in order to develop those positive, trusting bonds? It's one thing to know that we should do something; it's another thing entirely actually doing it – especially when you don't really know how.

As a senior teacher in a small student referral unit, I was well aware of this and spent a great deal of time trying to subtly encourage and advise other members of staff on how they could best get on with our more challenging students. Eventually I found that the simplest way of thinking about a relationship is as a kind of account – a relationship account, a bit like a bank account. When we want to grow the money in our bank account we make deposits and we get money back in the form of interest. So, the more money we put in, the more we get back out. In other words, we have to *give* in order to *receive*.

The principle is much the same with a relationship account – the more we put into the relationship account, the more we get back out. But we don't put in money (unless, of course, we're talking about the relationship with our own children). We make our deposits with something very different and much more valuable – we give ourselves. And we do it in two ways: by showing the other person we care about them and by communicating frequently with them.

If you think about the important relationships in your life – those with your spouse, your friends, your family – you will see that this is true. You simply cannot have a positive, flourishing relationship unless communication of some sort is taking place regularly. We are almost constantly connecting through speech (face to face, mobile, Skype, etc.) and the written word (text, letters, Facebook, email, etc.). We show we care by showing interest in each other's problems, helping each other, doing favours, saying nice things, giving gifts, going to the in-laws for lunch and so on.

By concentrating solely on these two essential factors – frequent communication and showing we care – I believe we have the simplest possible formula for building relationships with our students. We're going to be exploring multiple ways of doing this in this chapter.

If you doubt the efficacy of this, let me tell you another story about someone who used these two factors as the main tool for building positive relationships in his sales career – with dramatic results. Joe Girard used to be a car salesman and earned the title 'world's greatest salesman'. As you can imagine, you have to sell a lot of cars to reach the title of the greatest salesman in the world. Joe managed to do it a staggering 12 years in a row. He attributes his success largely to the relationships he had with his customers, and the way he went about building relationships with those customers is utterly fascinating yet remarkably simple.

Basically, all he did was this: whenever he met someone – in the street, in a shop, at a party, wherever – he would ask their name and address and enter them into his database. From that moment on, every month, these people would get a handwritten greetings card from Joe. Inside the card would be a brief but warm message along the lines of, 'Hey I was just thinking about you, Best wishes, Joe Girard' or 'Hey! I hope everything's going great for you, All the best, Joe Girard'.

At his peak, Joe was sending out more than 14,000 handwritten greetings cards *every month* – about 500 handwritten cards a day – and at that point he was employing three staff just to help him write them! Now, you might be wondering why a salesman would bother sending out all those cards, particularly when there was no mention of selling anything in them. All he was doing was keeping in touch and sending a warm greeting to people he barely knew. But think about this: most people change their car every few years. Who do you think was first in the minds of each of those 14,000 people when they next thought about replacing their vehicle?

You can see that Joe's formula for building relationships – communicating frequently with each person and then showing that he cared about them – matches ours perfectly. So let's find out how to apply these two essential factors to the classroom setting.

Frequent communication

As we've discussed, all relationships have frequent communication at their heart. You can't have a relationship of any kind unless communication is involved in some form, so it's not surprising we have poor relationships with our most challenging students. We're usually among the last people they would choose to sit down with for a nice friendly chat.

And besides, talking with them is actually very difficult – getting them to open up and start communicating is almost impossible in some cases, especially when you don't know them very well.

It's a vicious circle: you can't get to know them until you have something to talk about and you have little to talk about with them until you get to know them better. Clearly we need a subject they actually want to talk about so our first step is to find out their likes, hobbies and passions. We have more chance of getting them to talk with us if we talk about something which actually interests them.

Clearly, once you know their passions you can easily strike up conversation with them – you have a subject to chat about which will engage them. For example, if their favourite subject turns out to be mountain biking you could:

- Ask their advice about new bikes or related equipment. (We all like to be able to show how knowledgeable we are about a subject, particularly if it's our favourite one. Don't get me started about quinoa …)

- Share stories you've seen on television about mountain biking.

- Compile a list of websites on mountain biking and say, 'Here Jonny, you said you were into mountain biking – I found these websites you might like to look at …'

- Find relevant old books/magazines or newspaper clippings and offer them to look at in their spare time.

- Ask them about their bike or their riding adventures – perhaps they ride in competitions.

- Ask their advice on local tracks or courses.

- Take your own bike into school and ask them to show you how to fix it (young people love being given opportunity to show off their expertise).

- Sell them that old mountain bike you never got around to putting on eBay.

Now, we could just ask them what they enjoy doing in their spare time, and some of the friendlier students will be more than happy to tell us. But this method won't work with very angry, antisocial students – particularly those in their teens: 'So tell me, Jonny, what do you do at weekends?' 'Eh? It's nowt to do with you!'

We need to be a little less forward with these students and use methods that fly under their radar. I've found the following ideas to be very useful for discovering students' interests without getting their hackles up.

The record card questionnaire

I got this idea from my dear, late father. He was a wise man and his advice was always reliable so you can use it with confidence. Record cards are used by a salesman to record a client's personal information so he can be more familiar with his customer on his next visit. Each time he returns to the same client and has a conversation, the client reveals a little more about his interests and life in general, and this information can be added to the card. These titbits gradually build up and form a library of useful information which can be drawn on during the next meeting, and gradually the relationship deepens and develops as the client and salesman have more to talk about. It just speeds up the natural process of trust building and information sharing which would otherwise take much longer.

It's obvious to see that the salesman who does this will get on better with his client and probably sell more widgets into the bargain.

> Salesman A (who has spent time recording his client's personal details on his record card): Hey John, how are you this week? How's Lillian? You haven't forgotten her birthday on Friday have you? I brought you this booklet on carpet cleaning after your little accident last week. Now then, shall I show you this new line?
>
> Salesman B (who has taken no interest in his client): Hello Mr Smith. Would you like to buy our new product? No? Oh okay. Bye then.

Record Card Questionnaire

Tv & Film

What is the best film you've ever seen on DVD?

What is the best film you've ever seen at the cinema?

List 3 films you've recently seen that you enjoyed.
-
-
-

What are your 3 favourite TV programmes?
-
-
-

You can see from this that the record card is a great way of reducing the time normally spent getting to know someone. I have adapted this for classroom use by making it into a fun questionnaire for students to fill in – the record card questionnaire. They can complete this in registration periods, free periods, breaktimes, getting to know you sessions, social skills lessons or as an early finisher exercise. I used to give the questionnaire to new students at the start of term and let them fill it in as a first lesson exercise, a registration fill-in or as a wet break activity. The thing to remember is to give it them when they are in a reasonably good mood and when they have enough time to think about their answers.

Once you've got their completed questionnaires, go through the answers and pick out the main themes – the three or four key things they seem to be most passionate about – and record these in the teacher's notes box on the first page.

You can download a copy of the record card questionnaire from: www.noisyclass.com/bookresources.

The downloadable questionnaire is only a starting point – you may need to edit questions for your own use depending on the age group you're working with. I have used it successfully with students up to Year 10 (age 15) by phrasing the questions to suit.

So what do you do with the results? Here are a few ways you can use the information from the completed questionnaires:

- Increase the effectiveness of spontaneous rewards by tailoring them to appeal to students' interests. For example, if you have a student who is nuts about a certain breed of dog, there is no point in giving her a sticker with a picture of a tractor on it! (You'll find out more about spontaneous rewards in Chapter 6.)

- Provide appealing reading material for breaktimes, quiet reading sessions and registration – choose magazines, journals and books that relate to their specific areas of interest.

- Plan really interesting lessons. You might choose to prepare a series of lessons for the whole class around a topic that several students are interested in, or cover a skill such as narrative writing and encourage them to write a story about their subject of interest.

- Use them as a relationship building tool. They enable you to strike up conversations on a topic you know they are interested in and this is crucial with 'hard to reach' kids – it shows you care about them and are interested in them.

Suggestion box

Place a cardboard box on your desk and invite students to give you some information about their interests at the end of a session: 'On your way out, please write your favourite hobby/team/band/sport etc. on a piece of paper with your name on and leave it in the box on my desk.'

The way in

Okay, we've covered a couple of ways to find out about your students' interests, but as well as knowing their interests you need up your sleeve a way of starting the conversation with them too. Getting adolescents to open up and chat with you can be very uncomfortable – it often seems they would much rather do anything else but talk to you. For that reason we need a way in – and that's exactly what we're going to look at now.

Three ways to start conversations with students when they would rather not talk to you

1. Ask them for advice

When we give young people the chance to express their opinions it shows that we value them and what they have to say. So, when you're stuck for something to talk about simply ask your students questions that allow them to describe their interests and ideas – subjects they know about.

Some students love to give advice on music, fashion, hairstyles, make-up and jewellery, while others are keen on computer games, sports and pretty much anything practical or technical. You might ask one student for their opinion on what you should wear for an upcoming party or suggest a suitable CD for your own child's birthday. You might ask another for a run-down of the latest happenings on the current hot TV soap. Another student might be able to recommend a decent shop to buy a new bag for you or your spouse. If you're trying to strike up a conversation with a more outdoorsy type, try getting him or her to help you with something of a practical nature.

I once took my mountain bike into school with me and asked three of my new students to help me fit some parts to it at lunchtime. Prior to this I had really struggled to break the ice with these particular boys, but we never looked back after our 'cycle workshop' session. It was a great way to start a conversation and begin building a great relationship with them.

When it comes to talking about personal matters make sure it's their advice you're asking for, not their opinion. Asking a student what they think of your new hairstyle may set you up for ridicule, while asking them to suggest a decent hairdresser probably won't.

2. Ask a favour – the Franklin effect

When we think about ways to build bonds with people we intuitively think along the lines of doing something nice for them or caring about them – as per our second essential strategy for positive relationships. The 18th century politician, scientist and statesman Benjamin Franklin found an alternative, counter-intuitive approach which can be equally, if not more, effective in certain situations: asking favours of them.

To cut a long story very short, Franklin had apparently been trying to connect with a fellow politician but hadn't been able to – the other man wanted nothing at all to do with him. Franklin knew that this man happened to have a certain rare book in his personal library and he asked if he could borrow it from him. Surprisingly, the man's attitude towards Franklin changed completely from that moment on. In his autobiography, Franklin notes: 'When we next met in the House, he spoke to me (which he had never done before), and with great civility; and he ever after manifested a readiness to serve me on all occasions.'

Franklin attributed this to a simple principle: if you want to increase the likelihood of someone liking you, get them to do you a favour. I first came across this idea in Professor Richard Wiseman's fascinating book, 59 Seconds,[1] and if you think about it, it makes perfect sense – when you do someone a favour it

---

1   Richard Wiseman, *59 Seconds: Think a Little, Change a Lot* (London: Macmillan, 2009).

draws you towards them. Helping people gives us a sense of being needed or wanted which feels good.

So, the next time you're trying to make a connection and find a way in with a student, remember the Franklin effect. You could ask them to help you sort out a problem with your laptop, carry some heavy equipment, choose an outfit for a wedding, pick a CD for a teenage relative, help design a wall display, decorate your house, wash your car, do your ironing …

3. Give them a compliment

Apparently, when a person gives a compliment to a stranger, the person who has been complimented later describes that person as taller, slimmer and younger than they really are. That is great news – not only are compliments a great way to start conversations (as you'll soon see) but giving them has the added bonus of making you seem more attractive!

The problem with compliments is that they are often dismissed by the recipient because of self-esteem issues or perhaps because the compliment seems insincere or even manipulative. In that sense you might be forgiven for thinking they are a fairly useless way to start a conversation: 'Hi, I like your shoes.' 'Oh, thanks. Bye.'

To get over this hurdle, and take advantage of the opportunity compliments offer us in terms of starting conversations with our students, we just need to learn how to make them more believable. We can do this by adding just three pieces of information: (1) use the person's name to make it more personal, (2) add credibility by telling them why you're giving the compliment and (3) finish with an open-ended question.

> Hey Jonny, I like your shoes. My son would love a pair like that for his interview next week. Did you buy them around here?

> Hey Jonny, I hear you played very well in the match on Saturday. Mr Smith said you were very good in defence. What were the other team like?

And now you know the secret to giving great compliments you can use them in your private life too!

Showing that you care

The second of our key relationship building factors is showing students that you value them and care about them. The following collection of ideas will help.

Take time to learn their names

You must learn your students' names as soon as possible – not only does it make classroom time much easier to manage, but their name is the most important word they hear. I'm saddened when I think back to the students whose names I hadn't managed, or made the effort, to learn in my classes. As the year drew to a close there were still students I was referring to as 'you' with a pointed finger. What message does that give? You're not important enough for me to bother learning your name? It's quite shocking and disheartening when you look at it like that. Here's a quick way to make sure you never make the same mistake.

How to learn 40+ students' names fast

You can easily learn a class of 40 names in one lesson with this method. It's all just a matter of concentrating for a few minutes at a time on this single task and you'll be amazed how powerful it is.

Start by drawing a seating plan – a quick sketch of the layout in the room with enough space to write each student's name in the picture of their seat. Next, you need to get them all engaged in a settling activity. Give them each a simple and enjoyable ten minute task – any 'settling starter' will do (I'll explain what these are in Chapter 9). Each student needs to be sitting fairly quietly for around ten minutes without needing your assistance or attention – they should be able to just get on without your help while you add their names to the seating plan.

 Get a responsible student to add his/her classmates' names to your seating plan (i.e. write each student's name on the plan in the place they are currently sitting). This eliminates the chance of some students giving you false names which can happen when you're confronted by a 'streetwise' group.

Once that's done the fun starts. While the students are working, take a name from the seating plan and find the individual in the sea of nameless heads. All you do now is link a crazy image with their Christian name in your head. The weirder, bigger, more colourful, strange and humorous you can make this image the better. It should take no more than 30 seconds per person.

We remember pictures more easily than we remember names, and we remember odd, weird and funny pictures far more easily than ordinary ones. For example, if James is sitting at the front desk, an image that springs immediately to my mind is the Roald Dahl link – a giant peach. I would therefore spend a few seconds looking at James' face, imagining his head as a huge peach – complete with a few large insects eating their way out! Obviously, James wouldn't be aware that I'm doing this – although he might wonder why I keep smiling at him! Heather could be identified by the very messy heather bush on her head in place of her hair, with a swarm of bumble bees buzzing around her head. I might put Robert behind bars or in handcuffs, wearing a stripy shirt and eye-mask as a 'robber'.

For non-Anglican names the connections may be a little more abstract but the process is essentially the same. Sudeepa's name sounds a little like 'so deep' when I say it to myself, so I might imagine her standing on the edge of a lake or looking into a deep well. Muhammad, a very popular Muslim name, conjures up images of ancient Arabia for me, so I might see him adorned with long white robes and a head scarf. Alternatively, if he's a lively character, I might see him more as Muhammad Ali, wearing bright red boxing gloves. Adding personal characteristics such as temperament and hobbies to your linked image can be a big help when it comes to remembering names, particularly when you have more than one student with the same name and you have to distinguish between them.

Once you've learned your students' names in this way they will be cemented in your mind for good. Really simple, really works. And when you dismiss them all by name at the end of your first lesson together (without so much as a glance at your seating plan), the look on their faces is priceless.

Have massive expectations

In 1968, Rosenthal and Jacobson conducted a famous study which concluded that teacher expectations can have a positive impact on students' intellectual development.[2] In the same way that the Greek sculptor Pygmalion's high expectations became a self-fulfilling prophecy and turned a lifeless statue into a beautiful living being, the thoughts and beliefs we hold about our students can have quite dramatic effects on them.

To take advantage of this phenomenon, start by giving your students positive labels – try referring to them *all* (even the really challenging ones) as 'top students', 'excellent workers' or your 'favourites' – and you might find it helps them feel more positive about themselves (and behave accordingly). Constantly remind them that they are capable, they are good role models, they are likeable, they are wonderful, they are helpful, they are worthy of success and they can improve, providing they are willing to put in the effort.

2　See Robert Rosenthal and Lenore Jacobson, *Pygmalion in the Classroom* (New York: Holt, Rinehart & Winston, 1968).

As a teacher I knew that high expectations were important – it was in all the books, and most of the training courses and INSET[3] sessions I'd attended made mention of the fact. But it was only years later that I truly saw how powerful expectations are and the incredible effect (good and bad) they can have on young people.

I was once helping a friend to sell his house which I had been renting from him while he was abroad. One day, a well-to-do woman arrived at the door for a viewing. My computer, books and assorted paraphernalia were taking up most of the dining room and when she saw these she asked, 'What is it you do?' When I told her I was an ex-teacher and now helped teachers work with troubled kids, she gave me a pensive look and told me she had been a school failure herself and that her memories of her years in secondary school weren't very positive.

But she then went on to tell me that she was now one of the highest paid lawyers in the north of England. She explained that as a young girl she was an A* student. All through primary school she had been top of her class but when she reached secondary school it all went wrong – for two years (her important exam years) her attainment dropped significantly and she completely failed her O levels. She had to re-sit almost all of them. She passed her re-sits with flying colours (getting As and Bs) and went on to get excellent grades in her A levels. The rest is history.

'Wow!' I said. 'If we can find out what your magic recipe is for making such a massive improvement we could give struggling kids some powerful strategies for doing well in school.' But first I needed to know what had happened to cause her to fail for two years. And this was the astounding part. Initially she had no idea and was completely dumbfounded as to why she had never analysed this for herself before now – she hadn't given it a second thought. Now, however, she was as keen as I was to uncover the reasons for her fall and subsequent rise. In fact, we had both become so fascinated with the prospect that we had opened a bottle of red wine and completely forgotten about the house viewing!

Even after a torrent of probing questions from me (Did something terrible happen at home? Did you change schools? Did the curriculum change? Did you have

---

3   For those unfamiliar with the term, INSET refers to IN-SErvice Training which is compulsory staff training in the UK.

a problem with some of your teachers? Were you being bullied?) we were still no closer to finding out what caused her to go rapidly from a high achiever to failure – and then back again to success.

Then suddenly she remembered. After a year at secondary school her year group were put into sets and as a young girl she assumed the setting was based on ability. In reality the groups had been created simply to divide the year group equally – they were assigned by position on the register. Her surname began with 'W' and she now found herself – to her utter horror and dismay – in what she assumed was the bottom set!

From that moment on, she immediately lost all confidence in her ability and effectively became a bottom set student. Her grades plummeted and her school life took a terrible turn. Were it not for an assessment after her exams – presumably initiated by her devastated and shocked parents or worried teachers – which showed her true abilities, who knows where she would be right now.

Clearly, the beliefs students hold about their capabilities – affected to a great extent by the expectations their teachers have of them – can have a significant impact on their efforts in class. Children really need to know that someone in authority believes in them.

Offer plenty of support

I remember one young 15-year-old lad in a class I was covering many years ago whose behaviour truly pushed the envelope of unmanageability. The first lesson I had with Jake was a full-on battle of wits from bell to bell – he just would not settle, would not engage and was intent on wrecking the entire lesson.

I caught him next lesson at the door and asked him to wait with me while the other students went in. He thought he was going to get a rollicking for last lesson's performance and was rather taken aback when I said: 'You know what, Jake? Last lesson I couldn't help feeling there was something wrong – you didn't seem happy at all. I don't want you coming to my lessons and having a bad time. I don't want to be on your case having a go at you.' I smiled at him and he looked up at me as I continued, 'My lessons are supposed to be useful to you – I want you to get something out of them. Can you tell me what I can do to make it better for you, please?'

There was a long pause as he tried to make sense of what I was saying. Then he opened up, as if I'd turned a tap on. He began to tell me how he couldn't see the board, how he couldn't read very well and was supposed to wear glasses, how other students made fun of him if he did and how he didn't understand most of what was going on. His behaviour was the classic result of two of the most common de-motivators in the classroom – fear of failure and inadequacy.

We had to cut our conversation short so that I could get in to start the lesson, but those few moments outside the classroom were the beginning of a very different relationship between Jake and me. He now saw me as someone who was there to help him and I saw him as a young child with problems as opposed to a 'problem child'. I made a few changes to accommodate his weaknesses and gave him some extra support; his behaviour miraculously changed overnight. He arrived to lessons with a smile and his hand shot up almost every time I asked a question. The effort he put into his work from this point on was simply unbelievable.

Give them responsibilities

Often, our most challenging students are those with the greatest leadership potential; their behaviour is driven by a quest for attention and power and their strong personalities make them popular ringleaders. Giving them a responsibility is very fulfilling for them and saves them trying to gain notoriety in less appropriate ways. It also gives you, the teacher, very useful classroom allies.

Responsibility can take many forms – from being in charge of certain equipment through to monitoring and supporting more vulnerable members of the class (such as victims of bullying), keeping a group's noise levels at acceptable levels (such as the shushers we met in the introduction) or giving students the opportunity to grade their own work and choose lesson activities.

Here's a list of possible classroom jobs and responsibilities:

- Gofer – a student selected to run errands (go for this, go for that).

- Board monitor – responsible for cleaning the board and ensuring the surrounding area is tidy.

- Scribe – if you like to have your lesson objective and lesson instructions written up at the start of the lesson, this student can do it for you.

- Gardener – responsible for the upkeep of indoor plants in the classroom.

- Equipment monitor – responsible for keeping equipment trays tidy and complete.

- Noise controller/shusher – responsible for maintaining an orderly working environment and keeping their table group's conversation on track.

- Mr/Mrs Motivator – responsible for encouraging slow workers and keeping the mood in the room buoyant.

- Registration monitor – responsible for taking the register.

- VIP – welcoming new students and visitors and acting as a first port of call for other students who are experiencing problems of any kind. VIPs can also have special privileges such as breaktime refreshments, computer time, etc. The role can be awarded on a rotation basis or as a spontaneous reward for good effort. At one primary school I was working in recently, the VIPs were given high-vis workmen's waistcoats to wear as a uniform so they could be easily identified – they wore them with pride!

Cards and notes

Don't underestimate cards, notes and letters – they can be a very powerful way of connecting with some students, particularly those who are reluctant to talk face to face.

Cards, notes and letters show much more consideration and appreciation than spoken words. If it's a student's birthday, go a step further than just saying 'happy birthday' – help them feel special and give them a card (physically posting it home gets you bonus points).

Dear ...,

The work you did in class today was excellent. It's so nice to see you putting in more effort and you really can do well when you try, can't you? Come to think of it, you could do even better if you would get your homework in on time. Just in case you didn't write it down, tonight's homework is ...

If you need any help on it, come and see me before going home tonight so that we can make sure you do a good job on it. Let's make it 'your best ever homework'! I'll look forward to seeing you hand it to me on Wednesday. Have fun ...

Dear ...,

It was wonderful to see you in class today. The lesson always has a livelier atmosphere when you're around. ☺ For that reason it would be nice to see more of you. Can you make sure that you're in class on time tomorrow, please, so that I don't get worried about you? Remember, lessons start at 9.10 a.m. sharp. See you in the morning ...

If a student is ill, go a step further than simply marking them absent on the register – send a get well card. And if a student tries particularly hard or does something especially nice, why not give them a thank you card?

Marking work can be a chore but it's also another opportunity to connect, to strengthen bonds and to initiate communication with students who don't like talking face to face. By using sticky notes, or even writing directly in their books, you can ask them questions, send good wishes, congratulate them on an achievement, tell them jokes and give feedback of all kinds. These private little dialogues all work towards conveying the message that you care about and value them.

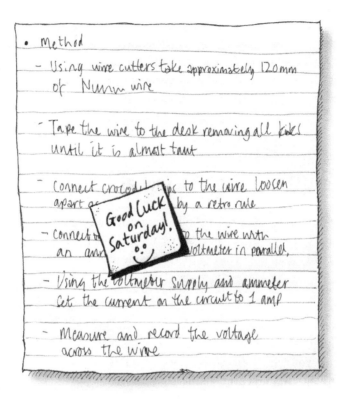

The comment in the picture above, for example, was a note I placed in the work file of a boy who was visiting his father for the first time in several months. He was apprehensive about the visit so the 'Good luck on Saturday' message was just a quick, personal way of giving him a bit of support. Often students respond to written comments by writing replies and a sticky note conversation develops – as does the relationship.

Make time to listen to them

Breaktimes and lunchtimes are a fantastic relationship building opportunity. A friend and teaching colleague of mine made a point of never spending his free time in school in the staffroom. Instead he spent breaktimes and lunchtimes in his room with his door always open. Students came in to play chess and board games or just to chat; he rarely, if ever, had a problem with classroom management. His reputation for 'being there' for the students, for being approachable, had spread throughout the whole school and all the students knew him to be easy to talk to and kind. He was greatly respected for that – even by the toughest students in the school.

Give or lend them something special

How many times does your most challenging student forget to bring a pen to the lesson? Instead of handing them a chewed old Bic pen from the pen graveyard, why not use this as an opportunity to build your relationship with them?

Lending them a cheap, tatty, broken pen says 'I don't think very much of you – I don't trust you enough to give you a decent pen and I don't think you deserve one', just as much as it says 'Everyone keeps nicking my pens and this is all I've got left'. But taking them to one side and saying, 'This pen was a gift from my son. I'm going to trust you with it because I know you'll look after it and I want you to write well today', gives an entirely different message.

Students respond to us in the way they feel they are being treated. Treat them with contempt and they will respond with indignation. Treating them with respect and giving them the clear message that you trust them will evoke an entirely different reaction.

Organise trips and visits

Taking your students out of the classroom environment brings a whole new dimension to your relationship with them. You naturally take on a more nurturing role in the eyes of your students which automatically suggests you care about them. Trips out, particularly residential trips, can also aid students' development of a wide range of social skills so relationships can be established and strengthened far more quickly than in a classroom situation.

Teach them new skills

We can show our care for a student by empowering them with skills to overcome their difficulties and shortcomings. I often use the example of a student who seldom, if ever, hands in homework. Does ranting at them help them correct their behaviour and do the required work? Could it be that the lack of effort is intensified by a lack of skills rather than pure belligerence? Students who frequently break rules or seem unwilling to follow them need support and education as much as they do discipline.

Spending some time teaching this student time management skills, or ensuring they understand the work sufficiently to complete it, will show a deeper level of caring than a detention ever could and may even help them to get their homework in on time.

Attend school events

If your students play a sport or perform in a concert or production of any sort, go and watch them. There aren't many better ways to show that you care about someone than giving up your free time to go and support them. Doing so also gives you a topic to talk about with them later in school.

Pay more attention to them

Make an effort to speak to every student each day and be sure to leave no one out of class discussions. Have a classroom photo-board and put up pictures of all your students – they can bring in their own from home or you can take pictures of them smiling and having fun in school. Pay attention to their health and if they don't seem well send them to the nurse/clinic. If they miss more than one or two days due to ill health, call home to see how they are doing or send a get well card and a pack of catch-up work with a note from the rest of the class. If it's their birthday, give them a cake and a card. If they are having a tough time at home, put a little note in their planner to wish them well. If they arrive at school with new shoes, a new coat, a new hairstyle or a nose ring, give them a compliment (you can always tell them to take the nose ring out after doing so). Little gestures like this will be remembered by your students for years – even a lifetime in some cases.

Perform acts of random kindness

If you've seen the film *Evan Almighty* (a funny and surprisingly good film with some powerful messages), you'll know that the word ARK (as in Noah's ark) stands for Acts of Random Kindness. The idea here is to try performing random acts of service or appreciation for your students to help them feel special. You can increase the effect by adding an encouraging note for them to 'pay it forward' (another great film) to other students. We've just mentioned one such act above – lending or giving them a special object of some sort – but this can be extended to giving additional time or going the extra mile to do something really special for a student or group. This is an excellent way to quickly change students' negative attitudes and can go a long way towards creating a very positive classroom community.

Here's an example of this which targets the whole group rather than individual students. It won't appeal to everyone reading this but it's very effective nonetheless. The idea is to go out of your way to be of total service to your class for a lesson or part thereof. And you can really go over the top with this – the emphasis should be on fun. For example, you could treat each student as if they were a 'guest' in your lesson – greet them politely by name at the door, seat them one at a time as if they are attending a fine restaurant and provide them with an unexpected gift of a pen or other equipment (plus the offer of a cushion if they are uncomfortable). Have soft music playing in the background and, while they are engaged in a nice activity, wait on them with soft drinks and a smorgasbord of sweets and treats to choose from, presented on a cake stand, of course. You could even dress up for the occasion and drape a wine waiter's towel over your arm. This certainly isn't a strategy for every lesson, nor for every group you teach, but as an impromptu way of saying thank you to a group who have made a big effort, or as an attempt to break the mood state of a difficult group, it takes some beating.

Display everyone's work

Classroom displays should feature the work of *every* student in the group. Granted, some students may not have completed work for inclusion and some hate seeing their work up on the walls; if that's the case, they can be given the chance to contribute to the display in other ways. One way is to put together a display making team. Arrange for someone from the art department (or an older/particularly artistic student) to give the group some tuition in display making skills such as lettering, colour, balance and so on, and give them the responsibility of managing and changing displays in your classroom. You could even hire the team out to other teachers at breaktime for a bit of extra cash.

Take the relationship challenge

Of all the strategies in this book this is probably one of the most powerful. Briefly, it involves making a definite commitment to improve relationships with any particularly hard to reach student who is causing you difficulties. That's not to say you ignore the others but that you make more of an effort with this one student for a set period of time.

The idea is to aim to spend a minimum of 30 seconds a day for 20 days (four working weeks) engaged in relationship building conversation with this particular student and then see how your relationship with them changes. If you find yourself doing more, even better. The target is just 30 seconds – more than that is a bonus.

Just to clarify, 'relationship building conversation' doesn't mean ordering them to sit properly in lessons or asking them why their homework hasn't been handed in; it's in addition to normal, day-to-day instructional conversation. You can talk about anything at all – TV, music, football scores, where they bought their cool new shoes, their hobbies/interests. If you find this difficult, remember to try any of the 'way in' conversation starters on pages 88–91.

Everyone can manage 30 seconds but it's going to take slightly more than a 'Hi, how's it going?' to fill it. On the days that you teach the student you will easily manage it during the lesson while other students are working, but on other days you will need to be more creative. It may mean actively seeking the student out in the lunch or bus queue, scheduling a weekly private 'How can I help you more with your work?' meeting, having lunch with them or just catching them in the corridor or outside your room before/after the lesson. There are countless opportunities to connect with students through the simple art of conversation – it's just a matter of taking advantage of them.

Note: Initially you will almost certainly encounter reluctance and negativity, and in some circumstances all this extra attention can actually freak out some students. All the strategies I've mentioned are great relationship builders, but if you go in too hard, too heavy and too fast you can find students running in the opposite direction.

We've all played the attraction–rejection game (the more attention we give to someone, the more they back away), so the trick is to tread carefully at first. If you go running up to a student with whom you've never connected and suddenly offer them a pile of magazines ('Here I got you these because I know you're interested in mountain biking!') and hit them with a load of personal probing questions out of the blue, naturally they are going to wonder what on earth is going on.

At best they will ignore you. At worst (particularly if you press too hard) they will think you're weird and all efforts to build a relationship from that point on will have a new obstacle – suspicion. So go easy and take it slowly, particularly with very challenging students.

You can download instructions for the relationship challenge from: www.noisyclass.com/bookresources.

Chapter 6
Positive reinforcement

Over the years I've noticed that teachers who find it hardest to manage student behaviour seem to be focused almost exclusively on what is going *wrong* in the classroom. They seem to be constantly on the lookout for students who aren't doing as they want. The best teachers spend more time looking for and acknowledging good behaviour, and in doing so create an entirely different, upbeat feeling in the classroom. It should be no surprise that these teachers tend to have fewer classroom problems to cope with.

In this chapter we're going to look at various positive reinforcement strategies used by successful teachers, starting with the most obvious one – praise.

The transformational power of praise

Let me share a little story to explain why I feel praise is one of the most powerful, transformational strategies a teacher can use.

I first started delivering behaviour management training professionally in 2006. Although I loved being in business for myself, after ten years or so in the classroom I found it very hard work. When I wasn't driving up and down the motorway or travelling abroad delivering training in schools and universities, I was spending virtually every waking hour wading through the various administration procedures (I am hopeless at paperwork of any sort) as well as trying to get the online part of the business running smoothly (I am equally hopeless at anything to do with computers). So, a large part of my life was being spent doing things I'm no good at which caused me no end of stress and frustration. Come to think of it, I suppose a lot of young people feel that way about school!

In those early days I would spend 12 to 18 hours per day working on the business and I would do that seven days a week, week in, week out to keep my head above water. I was in a perpetual state of anxiety from not being able to get things moving fast enough to meet the various monthly payments I was tied into, while simultaneously dealing with a computer which seemed to hate me.

After a couple of years I hit a brick wall. My mother was diagnosed with vascular dementia in 2008 and I found myself driving over to Cumbria from my home in Newcastle to help look after her three or four times a week, in-between caring for my teenage son (sorry, I forgot to point out that I was a failing single parent at the time). In addition, my father was suffering with leukaemia and Parkinson's disease and my sister's second kidney transplant had been rejected, leaving her on dialysis and in need of a third.

With all these issues on my mind and constraints on my time, the training bookings became sporadic and money soon started to dry up. On the odd occasion I was asked to run training in the south of England, I would sleep for a few hours in my car rather than book a hotel – partly to keep my costs down and partly so I could get back to help with my mother. It wasn't long before my own health started to suffer and I got to the point where something was going to have to give.

Obviously, my priorities were my family so I decided that I would have to shut down my business. I had put my heart and soul into it and giving it up would be like chopping off my right arm, but it had to go for the sake of my family and my sanity. Reluctantly I wrote an email to all my customers explaining the situation and my need to cease working. A lot of them were paying a small monthly membership fee in return for updates and new materials each month (which was now pretty much my sole income), but judging by the supportive messages I received most people understood. I shut down the shopping cart and took the website down.

After three or four months without an income things started to get very, very difficult. There is an old saying that you are only three pay cheques away from the gutter and believe me, there is a lot of truth in it. Because after three months the reminders and warning letters start coming in for things like mortgages and cars. And people start threatening to turn off your gas and electric. At one point I went for almost two weeks without any food in the fridge at all; I relied on friends helping me out with food parcels. Financially I was ruined and on more than one occasion I found myself hiding under the table from bailiffs who were knocking on the door. It was a tough time but I literally didn't have the headspace, the time or the energy to work.

Now, here's the interesting bit and the point of the story (thanks for sticking with me so far) … After a few months I did slowly start to get the business going again but what got me back on my feet wasn't what you might think. It wasn't the threat of having my electricity or gas cut off. It wasn't the fact that my car had been repossessed or even the danger of losing the roof over my head. The threats and punishments were not responsible for me changing my behaviour to start earning money again. (And yet how often do we threaten or punish kids, thinking this is the most effective way to get them to do what we want them to do?)

In my case the threats didn't work because I was too low to care. I had reached the end of my rope and had become quite depressed: 'Take the house, I really don't care. Take the car, it doesn't matter. I couldn't care less.' Again, this is the state of mind of many of our students. How many young people do you know who are genuinely bothered when they are threatened with yet another detention? 'So what? Do it, I don't care.' This is crucially important: when we get so low that nothing matters, punishment will not work as an effective motivator.

What got me sufficiently motivated to get back to work, and you can easily apply this method in your classroom with your students, was the complete opposite to punishments, penalties and pressure. Over a period of a few months I received literally hundreds of emails, letters and phone calls from customers telling me how much they missed my updates, how wonderful they thought the service I'd given them had been and how much they respected my decision to put my family first. I got emails from people saying I had transformed the way they teach and that I had indirectly affected the lives of hundreds of students in their care.

The support was incredible and I often think back fondly to the consideration and compassion I was shown by complete strangers. Unbelievably, several of these kind-hearted souls even offered to come to my house and help me in person to look after my dear mother! These were people with whom I'd had no contact other than sending them a few emails each week. It was staggering. Now, please understand, I am not saying any of this to brag. I just want to make clear the transformative power of positive feedback and support and the wonderful effect it can have.

You see, positive praise works on an *emotional* level. It goes far beyond the need to meet a target or show progression; it goes straight to the heart. And that's why it can cause deep changes in people very quickly. It has the power to literally change your most abhorrent students on the spot – as long as it's done well, so that's what we're going to look at in this chapter.

How to make praise more effective

As part of an exercise during my teacher training, I was told to keep a record of the frequency of positive statements I used during my teaching practice lessons. During an observation, my mentor listed any positive comments I made and anything that wasn't positive (not necessarily negative, just 'not positive'). When I looked at the results at the end of the lesson I was amazed.

Almost everything I had said during the lesson had been in response to students doing something wrong – 'Sit down,' 'Be quiet,' 'No, not like that,' 'Don't do that,' 'No,' 'When I say so,' 'Stop punching me'. My whole lesson was a continuous stream of corrections, instructions, commands and negative statements. And I discovered that I hardly ever acknowledged the students doing something right, seldom congratulated them on their efforts and that all my exchanges with students had a generally harassed, punitive edge.

There is plenty of research to back up the fact that students need more positive than negative interaction but it's irrelevant really. You need only put yourself in their shoes and imagine how you would feel receiving criticism after criticism to know the importance of positive feedback. So, after being made aware of my shortcomings in this department, I made an effort to address this during my next lesson.

I had read that making six positive statements for every negative one could bring about miraculous changes.[1] I tried it and the results were dismal. I found myself saying the same weak, cheap statements that you can hear behind every classroom door. You know the ones – 'Well done,' 'Very good,' 'Ooooh, excellent' – that kind of thing. Sure, I met my quota of so-called positive statements, just as I was advised, but what's positive about a teacher striding around the classroom spewing out throwaway comments like that? Especially when they are usually said with barely more than a sideways glance at the work to which they relate.

When we're talking about reaching students on an emotional level and creating lasting change, it's the quality of the praise we need to focus on rather than the quantity. There is a lot more to effective praise than just saying 'Well done', so in this section I'm going to share with you some ideas for making it really effective.

 ## Five ways to make praise and encouragement more effective

Here are some ways of improving praise so that it creates the kind of positive changes you want to see in your challenging students.

1. Make praise descriptive and specific

Real praise – the kind that actually makes a difference – comes from genuinely noticing when someone puts effort into something or has managed to complete something they wouldn't normally manage to do and then describing what they have done. Giving thoughtful, specific recognition demonstrates that you are taking real notice in what they are doing – in a way that a throwaway 'Well done' doesn't.

---

1   See Marcial Losada and Emily Heaphy, The Role of Positivity and Connectivity in the Performance of Business Teams, *American Behavioural Scientist* 47(6) (2004): 740–765.

If you want to improve the behaviour of students using praise, the comments you use must be in full recognition of what they have done right. By that I mean praise needs to be *specific* and *descriptive*. Like this:

> Jonny! Stand back and look at what you've done ... This is a fantastic portrait! What really sets this apart is the way you've made that eye come to life by showing the light reflecting here. That really makes it look realistic. And the texture you've got on the hair is superb.

> Jonny, you've sat quietly for the last ten minutes and got on with your work. That's great because I've been able to go and help other students and I haven't needed to speak at you or remind you to get on. Well done, you've shown you can work independently!

2. Praise effort rather than achievement

If a friend was dieting you wouldn't wait until they had reached their target weight before making positive comments, would you? You would help them along the way with encouragement because acknowledging their effort helps them stick in and persevere and, importantly, it can help them to overcome or avoid frustration.

By focusing on effort rather than achievement we can praise a student even if they fail, and that's very important. Waiting for a child to succeed in a task before praising them means missing out on untold opportunities to encourage them along the way.

Here are a couple of ways you can praise effort to encourage students:

> Jonny, you are working really, really well on this. What you've done so far is spot on. Just keep going using the same technique and you'll have it done in no time.

> You've tried so hard on this, Jonny. It's great to see you putting so much effort in – you've really showed tremendous determination and that's an important strength to develop.

3. Make praise sincere

Real praise comes from the heart (flattery comes from the teeth) and kids are very quick to spot someone who is just trying to manipulate them with fake positive comments. If you want real transformations to take place you have to make praise genuine – it's got to be sincere. That means you have to be hyper-vigilant to spot what might be very small positive improvements – just steps in the right direction. These are the things we need to jump on. We have to mark those moments because when we do, there is a good chance of them repeating that good behaviour.

4. Be aware that praise is often more effective on a one-to-one basis

Some students (a surprisingly large proportion) don't like receiving praise in front of other people, so you have more chance of your praise being well-received if you give it one to one in private. Catch them at the beginning of the lesson before they go into class, at the end of the lesson or in lesson time (but out of earshot of the rest of the students). It only has to be a short conversation but even 30 seconds giving some sincere, heartfelt praise is going to be time well spent.

5. Help them reflect on their efforts

Some teachers lavish praise on students for literally anything and everything in the hope that the sheer quantity of positive words will raise their self-esteem and motivate them. But praise is more effective when we get students to stop and reflect on what they have done. By getting them to pause and think about their efforts, we encourage them to recognise and evaluate the feelings associated with positive action. If they enjoy these feelings there is more chance they will want to repeat the actions – for themselves and not just to please someone else. One way we can do this is to simply ask a question about their efforts:

> Jonny, stop and look at your work a minute. Tell me what you think of what you've done today.

> Hey Jonny, now that everything has settled down, how do you feel to have got over that difficult problem? What skills did you use to resolve it? How does it feel knowing that you can use those same skills next time you are confronted with a problem like this?

Now that we know how to improve the praise we give to students, here are some methods to actually deliver it.

Four brilliant praise methods for the classroom

These powerful praise strategies can be used in the classroom and around the school to create change in your students.

1. Proximity praise (aka windscreen wiper praise)

Proximity praise relies on the 'ripple effect' where the positive feelings bestowed on individual students spread or ripple around the room. Other students then get the message that if they behave in a similar way, they too will receive positive attention and praise.

We can multiply the power of this effect with a novel idea suggested by a participant on one of my classroom management courses. It's called 'windscreen wiper praise' – it's very straightforward but also very effective.

Let's say Jonny is off task and not working as he should be. By praising two other students in class – the students sitting on either side of him, Kyle and Kieran – we use the power of proximity praise in a localised manner. If Kyle and Kieran are Jonny's friends it will make this even more effective but it works well regardless. This is one possible scenario:

> Hey, Kieran, you've got it. I honestly didn't think you'd manage that question. Absolutely brilliant – it's good to see you learning.

> Let's have a look at yours, Kyle … you've really improved. You've got that bit right, well done. Now, how could you improve this bit and get to the next level?

A moment later …

> Thank you for putting that in the bin, Kyle. By the way, I saw that film last night you were talking about – it was really funny. Thanks for suggesting it.

> Nice one, Kieran. I like what you've done there. I'm really pleased with you two, you're working very well. Thank you.

The process is repeated several times.

Do you see how it works and have you guessed where the name 'windscreen wiper praise' comes from? The idea is that as a result of the teacher continually engaging with Kyle and Kieran, Jonny's head will be going from side to side wondering what his two neighbours have done to attract all this positive attention. It's likely that he will want some too.

2. Indirect praise

Indirect praise is a great way to acknowledge a student's strengths, abilities and efforts without saying anything to them directly. Often, it can be more impactful (and easier for the student to accept) hearing teachers saying nice things about them to other people rather than to their face.

There are two ways of doing this. The first is to praise a student to his classmates. In this example, the teacher acknowledges a student's efforts by telling other students in the class about their work. In each case the statements would be spoken just loud enough for Jonny to hear.

> Go and ask Jonny about this bit – he's picked it up very quickly.

> Go and watch Jonny for a minute – he's brilliant at this and you can learn a lot from him.

> Go and ask Jonny if you can have a look at his answer from last lesson – it was exactly what I was looking for.

The alternative is to praise a student to a member of staff. This time, you report the student's efforts and abilities to another member of staff just within earshot of the student, as if you're not aware they are listening. Students love to discover that members of staff talk positively to each other about them.

Did you see what Jonny did this morning, Mr Smith? Honestly, I can't believe how hard that lad is trying – what a turnaround.

3. Written praise (the students' favourite)

I've surveyed hundreds of students at all ages over the years and asked them which form of positive acknowledgement/reward they most like to receive in return for good work/effort. I give them a list (e.g. take their work to a senior teacher, have work put on display, get mentioned in assembly, contact with home, get a merit mark, have a comment written in their book, stickers, candy/sweets, time on the computer, choice of activities) and ask them to tick the one they would prefer.

Surprisingly, the one which comes up top almost every time is contact with home, and from experience I've found that sending a positive letter home or making a short telephone call to parents/guardians can quickly transform a previously negative child into one who is far more motivated and eager to please. This method works well with all age groups (up to age 16 and beyond). It is also very effective for students who don't accept public praise very well – a letter home means their friends will never find out!

Letters home can be quick notes or more formal letters on school headed paper. You can send out simple postcards for odd pieces of particularly good work or award 'extra special' letters in response to sustained effort. I find generic pre-printed notes – the type you buy in 'praise pad' format too insincere. It's much better to use typed, personalised letters, and the best way to organise these for speed and ease is to have a copy of the following letter template (or similar) ready written in a file on your computer.

Date

Dear _____,

I just want to inform you that _____ was a delight to teach today. He/she worked hard, and behaved well and was a pleasure to have in the class. You should be very proud of him/her.

Yours sincerely,

Mr Smith

Teacher of (subject)

It's then just a matter of typing in the name, setting the correct gender, printing it out on headed paper and either giving it to the student to take home or (better) posting it out to their home address. You can always add a little more flavour to the template depending on how much time you have at your disposal and what sort of mood you're in.

4. Student generated praise – the 'You're great!' sheet

The 'You're great!' sheet is a lovely way to get students used to the idea of giving praise and receiving it from each other. It consists simply of five 'You were a great team member because …' prompts and one copy is given to each member of a table group or learning team.

Members of each team then take it in turns to write a positive comment about each of their fellow teammates before folding the paper (thereby hiding their comment) and passing the sheet on to another student. In this way, each student receives three or four inspiring comments relating to a different attribute or skill.

I first came across this idea when working as an activity instructor with a group of young offenders at an outdoor centre in the Lake District. The centre manager introduced the sheet at the end of a two day walking expedition and it was really touching to see the comments these young people wrote about each other. I think one of the reasons it works so well is because adolescents often find it hard to say what they feel, so being able to write comments, anonymously if they prefer, frees them up to say what they really admire about each other. Also, each student leaves the session with a written record of these compliments to look back on. Sadly, spoken words are often soon forgotten whereas written comments can be kept for a long time.

I first started telling teachers about the 'You're great!' sheet around ten years ago, and I've heard lots of wonderful stories during that time of students being so pleased with the comments they've received that they've kept these bits of paper for years!

 You can download a copy of the 'You're great!' sheet from: www.noisyclass.com/bookresources.

You're Great

Team Member Name:

One thing we must always do when working with other people is show appreciation for their efforts. After your activity, fill in this form for each member of your team.

1. Write your name in the box above and pass the form to one of your teammates. They will fill in one of the blanks and then pass the form on to another teammate to fill in another of the blanks. You will get your completed form back once everyone on your team has added a positive comment to your form.

You were a great team member because ...

From: _____

You were a great team member because ...

Seven creative positive reinforcement methods

Positive reinforcement isn't just about giving verbal praise and encouragement; it helps if there is some variety in the way you acknowledge appropriate student behaviours. With that in mind, here are some creative ideas for marking the moment. Each one is guaranteed to raise the spirits in any classroom.

1. The victory dance

Teach students to develop their own personalised ten second 'victory dance'. Whenever you want to offer special praise to a student, clear a space at the front of the room (or install a podium if you have spare budget), pump up the bass and allow them their ten seconds of fame!

2. Wooo! cards

Issue all students with a special 'Wooo!' card (a laminated piece of paper or card with 'Wooo!' written on it). Whenever a student performs particularly well in class or manages to complete something they have struggled with in the past, call out 'Wooo!' and have everyone else hold up their 'Wooo!' cards while shouting 'Wooo!' back at you.

3. Silent cheers

Teach students to reward fellow class members for good work and good behaviour with a silent cheer. Offer spot prizes for the most dramatic and convincing exhibition of silent applause. This is particularly useful during exam periods or when the teacher in the neighbouring classroom has expressed concern about the amount of fun your classes seem to be having.

4. Wiggly wooos

A slight variation on 'Wooo!' cards. Every time you say, 'That deserves a wiggly wooo', students wave their fingers in the direction of the student in question and call out 'Wooo!' in unison.

5. And the winner is ...

Throughout the week be on the lookout for students doing good work, good deeds, improved effort and so on. Every time you see something positive, scribble the student's name down on a piece of paper, together with a very brief reminder of their behaviour, and place it in a jar or container on your desk. At the end of the week, draw a few names from the jar and hand out surprise prizes to the winners (see also 'wacky awards ceremonies' below).

6. Wacky awards ceremonies

Before your wacky awards ceremony takes place, you first need to create a 'wall of fame' on which to display extra special work completed by students. This need be nothing more elaborate than painted brick effect paper (you can get the students to make this) stuck on an area of wall or over a display board.

Next, you need the awards and trophies. These could be gold discs (old vinyl records sprayed with gold paint and with the title of the work/award on the label), over-sized rosettes, chocolate medals covered with gold shiny paper, cheap plastic trophies and so on.

With these in place you can now hold wacky awards ceremonies at the end of the week or as a conclusion to a scheme of work. Trophies and awards should be presented to students with as much drama as possible (think Academy Awards ceremony) and their work can then be displayed on the wall of fame.

7. Staffroom praise board

This is a whole school approach to building a positive working environment as well as helping to develop positive relationships between all staff and students. It is based on the principle that individual students' efforts often get overlooked, particularly in a large setting. This strategy ensures that even the smallest improvements made by individual students are noticed and acknowledged, potentially by every member of staff.

First, assign an area of wall in the staffroom for the praise board. There should be room for five to ten A4 sheets and it should be an area which staff will see whenever they enter the staffroom. Each week students are nominated for a place on the praise board (they aren't told about this). Staff put forward a student and give reasons for their nomination. After a vote, a photo of each chosen student is put on the board together with a brief summary of why they have been selected.

The idea is that every member of staff will see this board regularly throughout the course of the week. When they next spot one of the students from the board – either in the classroom, in the dinner queue or out in the yard – they can mention how impressed they are with their achievement. Over the space of a week, a student will receive a huge amount of positive, and often much needed, reinforcement with several members of staff acknowledging the same achievement.

Hey Jonny, I hear you were very good in maths this week. Well done, mate, keep it up!

> Great work, Jonny! A little bird told me you managed to get through a whole day without being sent out of a single lesson. Brilliant! Isn't it better when you're not getting a detention every day?

The danger of using rewards for positive reinforcement

The most commonly used motivational strategies in schools usually involve some kind of reward programme where, typically, points and prearranged prizes are awarded to students as they make progress along a chart or towards a points total.

I have worked in several settings where programmes like this have had a very positive, almost miraculous, effect, particularly on the behaviour of students. Sadly, these effects were always short lived for a significant percentage of the students they were set up to help and their efficacy waned with time.

No matter how elaborate or brightly painted the star chart and no matter how fantastic the prizes, some students will either become bored or frustrated with the system or the prearranged rewards. For many students, rewards are just not a suitable long term strategy. One of the main problems with reward programmes is that they don't take into account students who lack the capacity or skills to complete a designated task or meet a required level of work. They just assume that the only reason they aren't working is because they don't want to.

For example, if you offer a group of teenagers a crisp £5 note each to copy some numbers and letters from the board, most of them will be finished in no time. But if you offer the same £5 reward in return for performing some advanced algebra with the numbers and letters they have just copied down, you will get a much different result. Those who have the skills to do the task may work a little harder to get the reward, but for those who don't have a clue about algebra the reward won't help at all. If anything, seeing other students happily working their way towards some extra money for the weekend – when they have no hope of doing so – will only add to their frustration.

Similarly, what about a student who is offered a reward to bring in his homework? If he lives in an acutely chaotic home where school is viewed negatively by other family members and he has never been taught even the most basic of time management skills, the reward won't help him. It won't make his family members support him and it won't teach him the required organisational skills to make the time to sit down to do his homework.

You can probably find a simple example of this in action in your own life too – whenever you lose a personal item, for instance. The prize or reward is finding the lost item, and if it's a particularly valuable or treasured item then the prize is great. Yet no matter how much you want to find the item, if you don't know how or where to find it, you're at a disadvantage. Your valuable reward can't improve your ability to locate it.

During courses I often use the promise of cash rewards for a series of impossible tasks to hammer home this message. Participants are offered increasingly valuable cash prizes if they manage to complete a series of puzzles. But they can't do it, no matter how much they want to. It makes no difference how much I increase the prize fund either – they can't complete the task because they don't have the required knowledge. Bottom line: if the skills are lacking, the reward won't work.

Another problem with rewards is that they can divert attention from the actual task in hand. When the reward itself becomes the goal, the student loses interest in the task and is unlikely to feel any benefit or derive any joy from completing it for its own sake. Also, when a student becomes fixated on an incentive in this way, they become reliant on the view of the teacher or whoever is responsible for giving the reward, and therefore independence isn't promoted.

It's bad enough that rewards can stifle independence and lead to arguments but the biggest problem has to be that they only have a temporary impact. Once the treats (or the person giving the treats) have gone, the negative behaviour resumes. At worst they help to build and sustain a society of young people who will only do as they are asked as long as they are given something of value in return: 'Sure, I'll do as you ask but what's in it for me? What are you going to give me?'

Do we want a society like that? Of course not, so we need to get away from relying on rewards based systems. Our aim must be to teach appropriate behaviour and encourage students to behave appropriately for the right reasons and for the intrinsic rewards such behaviour brings – not because they have been promised a nice treat.

Despite these qualifications, rewards themselves aren't *all* bad if offered wisely – we just have to get the timing right. You see, when rewards are promised in advance ('Do this and I'll give you this') they are nothing more than bribes. But when they are unexpected and are given after an increased effort or positive change in behaviour, they can mark the moment very well and reinforce the behaviour we want to see.

Student effort should be recognised and celebrated, and rewards can be used to this end. But we can do better than to rely entirely on bribery where treats are promised in advance of an achieved target, as is the case with most school reward systems. Let's look at a better way to use rewards as true motivators – offering them spontaneously as occasional surprises.

The right way to use rewards

Gifts, presents and favours are always pleasing to receive but they have far more impact when they are a total surprise. One of the most effective reward systems I ever saw in operation in a school worked entirely on this basis. Unlike most other centres and special schools I had worked in for children with behavioural difficulties, there were no formalised reward systems in place here – there were no sticker charts or points totals leading to 'golden time' or the obligatory range of treats and prizes at the end of the week. Instead, students who had shown improved effort were given pleasant and unexpected surprises.

A surprise might be a trip into town, a visit to a park or sports centre or to an event or show, helping out with unpacking some deliveries, lunch at a cafe with a youth worker or even lending the caretaker a hand with some gardening. It all depended on the student's interest and the level of reward the teachers felt they deserved.

I know surprises like these are impractical for most comprehensives and larger schools, but part of the effectiveness of this approach was in the method of delivery rather than the reward itself. A member of staff (a youth worker, assistant or another teacher) would walk into the classroom (this was prearranged with the class teacher) and say something along the lines of: 'Jonny, I hear you've been working very hard this week. I think you deserve to come out with me today – we're going for a trip to the garage.'

The impact this had on the other students (and Jonny, of course) was quite astounding. There was no build-up or expectation on the students' part, but good effort was most definitely rewarded. The set-up gave the opportunity for the teacher to say, 'Look what happens when you work hard', and it was a profound moment for the other students to see Jonny walk out of the room for his treat. Individual spontaneous rewards like this are most effective when they mean something to the student. This is one reason why it is so important to get to know students and find out their hobbies and passions.

The following spontaneous rewards can be adapted to fit any individual student's interests, although some of them are applicable to younger children only.

Classroom privileges

The individual rewards listed below may seem small and insignificant compared to the expensive tangible prizes (record vouchers, mobile phone vouchers, etc.) offered in some school reward systems, but if chosen wisely and delivered at the right time, and in the right way, they can have a positive and lasting impact on students.

- Sit at the teacher's desk.

- Time on the computer.

- Be first in line for lunch (or can nominate a friend).

- Classroom job – taking care of the class animal(s), being in charge of materials/supplies, watering plants, taking the register, operating the whiteboard, etc.

- Have lunch with the teacher (or head teacher).

- Use specific materials/equipment – special pens/paper/computer program, etc.

- Show visitors around the school.

- Be a helper in the room with younger/less able children.

- Help the secretary.

- Help the librarian.

- Invite a friend from another class into the room for lunch.

- Take a class game home for the night.

- Keep a favourite soft toy/class mascot on your desk.

- Use the couch or beanbag chair.

- Set up a display.

- Be leader of a class game.

- Get a worksheet from the 'fun pile'.

Special awards and trophies

Awards are almost always used in classrooms in the form of certificates, but why stop there? A trophy is far more appealing – even if it is just a flimsy, plastic joke 'Oscar' – and it doesn't have to be something the students take home. It's the recognition and the ceremony that counts. A very brief, simple, humorous, surprise award ceremony can take place spontaneously to highlight students' progress in any given area – for example:

- Today's Independent Worker award goes to … (suggested joke trophy: toy plastic workman figure).

- This week's Early Finisher award goes to … (suggested joke trophy: toy plastic watch).

- Today's most improved student is … (suggested joke trophy: rosette or certificate).

- This week's Mrs Mop award for tidying the room goes to … (suggested joke trophy: a duster or scrubbing brush).

- Today's Mr Motivator award for keeping everyone positive goes to … (suggested joke trophy: cheerleader's pompom or whistle).

Work related rewards

- Allow them to show work to a younger class – as an example of the excellent work these students will be producing as they move up through the school.

- Ask the head teacher to come in and look at the student's work (or send the student to the head teacher's office with their work).

- Put the work on a special 'wall of fame' noticeboard reserved for the very best work each week or on a special display board near the school entrance.

- Make an arrangement with a local paper/free sheet publisher to feature 'excellent school work' and allow the student to send their work in for publishing.

- Compile a class/school newsletter and feature a collection of the best work in it each week/month.

- Send the work home to parents or invite parents in to see it.

- Put up a website or blog for excellent work to be displayed.

Trips and excursions

- Lunch off site.

- Accompany a teacher to 'advise' him/her on a special purchase – for home or school use.

- Museum, library or exhibition related to the student's particular interests.

- Any work-related visit associated with the student's hobby or interest (e.g. football ground, bicycle shop, beauty salon).

- Park, swimming pool, sports centre, ice rink, etc.

- An errand to help a member of staff.

- A visit to a hospital, care home, dogs' home, etc. to do voluntary work.

- Involvement in a local environmental 'clean up' project.

The golden ticket

This is a very special spontaneous reward. The golden ticket creates a moment of buzz, intrigue, excitement and expectation which gets students talking, puts a smile on their faces and has them returning to lessons in a great mood – thus doing no harm at all to your status as their favourite teacher.

The golden ticket can be used to represent a huge variety of pleasurable experiences for your students, with the proud winner being even luckier than young Charlie Bucket himself. The lucky ticket holder could be entitled to such things as early lunch, a no-homework night or five minutes of a preferred activity (e.g. computer time, drawing, playing a game, eating a snack, having a cup of tea, watching a film).

 If you're wondering where you might procure a shiny, glittering, realistic looking golden ticket, then you need look no further than the online resource area which accompanies this book. You can download a golden ticket reward template from: www.noisyclass.com/bookresources. Just print one out on yellow paper, add some gold glitter and hey presto!

The million pound behaviour note

Here's another very quirky reward you can give your students when they do something extra special. The million pound behaviour note (also available in dollars and euros) is a cool reward you might want to give out now and again when your students surprise you by making progress in terms of behaviour. Like any reward, the novelty value will wear thin over time but you might just find, for a while at least, that these little slips of paper will prove very popular and bring a new level of eager compliance to your classroom!

You can download a copy of the million pound behaviour note from: www.noisyclass.com/bookresources.

Part 2

A step-by-step lesson with the noisy class

Chapter 7
Taking control at the door

I believe good classroom management starts outside the classroom. If a group of noisy, out of control young people are allowed to fall into the room, pushing, shoving, shouting and messing around, you're going to have to spend a good deal of time settling them down and getting them ready to learn. More importantly though, from a psychological point of view, they are going to be feeling as if *they* are the ones in charge, entering your teaching space on their terms. Once this imbalance of power has been established it is very difficult to regain control, and this is where a lot of problems lie for struggling teachers – students will totally ignore a teacher who they perceive not to be in charge.

An important step in succeeding with the really tough group, therefore, is to take control at the door. And the manner in which you do this is crucial. When I first started teaching I basically had one very ineffective strategy at my disposal for managing behaviour. If they didn't do as I asked, I shouted at them. And if they still didn't do as I asked, I shouted a bit louder. Eventually I was shouting at the top of my voice and the kids were just gawping at me.

You can't get control just by barking orders at this group and then expect them to stand to attention like well-trained soldiers. Yelling at them only gives tough students more reasons to hate you. It gives the argumentative ones an excuse to answer back. It puts the wallflowers on the defensive. It conveys the message that you have lost control, and it raises your blood pressure.

There is not a single person who benefits from you yelling and shouting, and when you use any kind of aggressive approach with young people (even frowning can be interpreted as an act of hostility by some students) you're going to establish a negative 'them and us' atmosphere before they walk through the door. When this happens, it's almost guaranteed that your lesson is going to be a battle.

So, a difficult group needs to be calmed down g-r-a-d-u-a-l-l-y. By establishing a calm, welcoming atmosphere at the door you set the tone for the rest of the lesson. And then, once they are in a more relaxed state in which they are more likely to listen, you can tell them what to do with a much better chance of them actually doing it.

 ## How to get students calm and settled at the door

There are two steps to quietening the students at the door.

1. Make general, non-confrontational statements as to the behaviour you want to see rather than confrontational rants about things you don't want to see

In most disruptive classrooms the teacher focuses on what is going wrong. It's easy to constantly complain about students, moan at them for not behaving exactly as we want them to and to slip into blaming them or accusing them of doing things wrong. But this creates a very negative atmosphere which has a huge impact on the behaviour of the students and actually makes things worse for us as teachers.

If you want students to respond positively to you, do the opposite. Focus on what students are doing right – thank those who are doing as you've asked and then calmly remind the others to do the same. By reinforcing the behaviour you do want to see, you will quickly create a positive, warm atmosphere in which the majority of students naturally start to settle, rather than an oppressive, angry situation which puts everyone on edge.

Here's how *not* to do it:

> CONNOR! STOP TALKING AND STAND AGAINST THE WALL. NOW! LIAM! WHY ARE YOU ALWAYS LATE? SHUT UP KYLE! YOU TWO, COME HERE NOW!

And how to do it:

> Thank you Jonny for standing quietly and you Chantelle, thank you. Thank you Liam for settling down. Thank you Connor. This group here is nice and quiet – thank you girls. Let's settle down now over here. There are still a few people shouting and messing about. We can all go in as soon as everyone is standing still without talking. Thank you Wayne, nice to see you ready to go into the lesson. We're just waiting for a few others now – we'll go in as soon as everyone is quiet.

Notice also in this example that we don't name those who aren't yet quiet. There are no personal accusations here because the minute you name and shame a student you set yourself up for an argument. Instead we make general observations ('there are still a few people talking and messing about,' 'we're just waiting for a few others now') and give gentle positive reminders ('we'll be going in as soon as everyone's quiet').

2. Chat informally with individuals and small groups of students

I mentioned in Chapter 1 the idea of 'divide and conquer' as an aid to managing lively and rebellious groups. If you try to address a noisy class at the door en masse it's very difficult to get everyone's attention, and if you don't manage it you lose credibility straight away. A better way is to focus on speaking to small groups and individual students.

Teachers who are comfortable chatting informally with their students outside the classroom – in the bus queue, at lunch, in the yard and in the corridor – tend to get much more respect from them and find their students responding much more positively to them. Spending just a few minutes talking, mingling and socialising with your students in the corridor goes a long way towards helping to set the right tone for the lesson and really helps settle students down. Importantly, it lets them see that you are relaxed and in control in their presence. Timid teachers and those who worry they are going to struggle with the group avoid mixing with students and give the clear message that they are basically scared stiff of them.

Of course, infiltrating student cliques and getting individuals to chat with you can be difficult, particularly when your relationship with them isn't established, but there is one thing I can suggest beyond the relationship building tools we talked about in Chapter 5. It comes down to exactly what my first teaching mentor advised me to do – get into 'kid culture'. Watch the films and TV programmes they watch, listen to the music they listen to and show interest in all the other things that dominate their world. In this way you'll be able to contribute to and initiate conversations on all kinds of worthwhile and stimulating topics, like *iCarly* and *Family Guy*.

Another advantage of spending a minute or two with your students at the door is that you get to spot any likely problems and troublemakers. You know the kind of thing – students who have been arguing, messing around, hyperactive, upset, mischievous and so on in the playground or corridor are highly likely to continue this behaviour in your classroom unless you do something about it. Most potential problems are easy enough to spot once we're tuned in to looking out for them. Students who won't remove their jackets/hoods, who are huddling in groups whispering, pointing and giggling, who are using mobile phones and carrying hand grenades are all cause for concern.

I don't need to tell you what to look for, but the key is that you do need to be vigilant and you must be prepared to deal with any student who doesn't respond positively to you at the door. For example, if Jonny is normally a chirpy soul but turns up for class without his trademark smile and fails to return your greeting, you know something is wrong. It may be prudent to spend a little time with him one to one to find out what is troubling him before you let him in the classroom.

The main thrust of this approach is prevention. It's about spotting and dealing with problems as early as possible in order to stop them from escalating. As we've already discussed, when you're addressing a student on a one-to-one basis, particularly about issues of a sensitive nature, it is crucial that you do so quietly and caringly and out of earshot of other students.

Here are some suggestions for what to say to a student who looks unsettled or agitated at your classroom door:

Teacher: Jonny, you look a little excited today, what's up mate?

Jonny: Nothin.'

Teacher: Oh cool. I was just a bit concerned because I don't want you getting worked up. Listen, I know you sometimes struggle to keep yourself calm in this lesson so here's what I'll do … I'll keep a special eye on you and if I see you starting to get too lively I'll come and have a quiet word. That way, I won't need to tell you off in front of everyone else – we'll just keep it between the two of us – a sort of 'early warning system' to keep you out of trouble. Okay? Is there anything else you want me to know about?

Or:

Teacher: Oh that's good. I was just a bit concerned because I don't want you getting wound up. Listen, I know you sometimes struggle to keep your temper in this lesson so here's what you can do … Any time you feel yourself getting irritated or frustrated, just put this blue card on the corner of your desk or hold it up in the air for me to see. That way, I'll be able to help you before things get out of hand and without any of the other students knowing. Okay?

Note: If you're faced with a particularly agitated student, see 'Dealing with problems' on page 217 for a more detailed approach.

When issues come up they must be addressed before you let the students into the room, because if they are going into the classroom with unanswered concerns they will almost certainly cause problems and disruptions down the line. Obviously, some problems are easier to deal with than others so here's a useful stock response to use for an issue that can't be sorted out on the spot:

Jonny, I can see why that is a concern for you. It's not something I can help you with right at this moment because I have a lesson to run, but I'm glad you've made me aware of it. I will help you with this but it will have to be straight after the lesson. Put it to the back of your mind for now and we'll sort it later.

This process of settling students down at the door shouldn't ever turn into a game in which the students just string you along because you're being 'nice' to them. As you well know, a tough group will walk all over a teacher who doesn't convey an air of control, and if this period of chatting and mixing with students goes on too long it will backfire – the group will become more and more boisterous and difficult to control. To prevent this from happening, keep the time you spend outside the classroom to no more than a minute or two before you start filtering students into the room.

So, the class is lined up, calmed down and ready to go into the classroom. Now we need to sidestep a moment to discuss where they will be sitting.

Chapter 8
Seating plans

A properly thought out seating plan is an essential tool when you're faced with a very challenging class. I remember, early on in my career, what it was like trying to change the seating with some of the tougher groups. They argued so much about not being allowed to sit with their friends that I ended up scrapping the new plan before the lesson was over and letting them sit where they wanted. It all boiled down to the fact I didn't want the confrontation. It didn't work, of course; my early lessons were chaos.

Eventually, by sticking to my guns and imposing the seating plan despite the many complaints and cries of 'But I don't like so and so' and 'I'm *not* sitting with him/her', I soon noticed a huge improvement in behaviour. After a few days my classes settled down. The students got used to their new seats and, more importantly, they started to understand that I was the one in charge.

The classroom is *your* room and as such *you* make the decisions – including those regarding seating. Yes, when you introduce a new seating plan there will probably be uproar at first. Some will sulk, some will try to sneak back to their original seat, some will boldly march to their original seat and some will refuse to move altogether. And almost all of them will complain in one way or another. But stick with it. Refuse categorically to entertain any requests or pleas because bending the rules for one student will ruin your plan and leave your classroom in meltdown. Ride the storm; on the other side of the tantrums there is a calm(er) sea.

As you've hopefully noticed by now, a huge part of the 'take control of the noisy class' approach is to pre-empt classroom problems and have solutions ready and waiting up your sleeve. It's inevitable that some of your students are going to complain about your seating plan so here's a response you can use.

How to deal with complaints about seating plans

Start by saying to your students:

> We all like to sit with our friends but I want you to succeed. Let's try this: write down the name of two people in this class who you feel will *help you work* – this may be because you feel they won't distract you or they will be able to help you if you get stuck. I will then set the seating plan so that, where possible, you are sitting with at least one of these people.

Get the students to write these names down on a sheet of paper with their own name at the top. This gives them some limited choice in the seating arrangement which is easier for them to accept than having no choice at all.

Next, and this bit is optional, put a calendar on display showing the number of lessons left in the term and tell the group that as long as they work quietly and respectfully, you will change the seating plan after another X lessons. In this way, as long as they behave appropriately, they will have the opportunity to enjoy a number of lessons sitting with their friends.

A seating plan that works – cooperative learning teams

Some teachers are advocates of seating students in boy–girl rows or pairs facing the front because they feel this reduces opportunities for interaction and, of course, disruption. Personally, I don't like this type of seating arrangement and I don't think students do either, so they might kick up more of a fight if you try this. If you want a proven, realistic, long term method for increasing engagement, which facilitates positive peer interaction, promotes social skills development and reduces disruption, try seating your students in table groups instead.

Specifically, you should aim to group your students in what we can call 'cooperative learning teams'. Generally, a cooperative learning team is made up of four students – a high achiever, a low achiever and two middle achievers. Where possible it will include males and females and, where appropriate, ethnic groups will also be equally represented.

There are four key benefits to seating your students in cooperative learning teams:

1. Positive peer relationships are developed. As a result of students helping each other to reach work targets and other common goals they build strong bonds. As the sense of community grows there are fewer arguments and fewer disagreements between students. It can be quite amazing to see your toughest students become nurturing as they help other members of the group.

2. Lower achieving students gain confidence and motivation. By working collaboratively with higher achieving students, lower achieving students are able to take part in activities without feeling they lack the necessary skills and understanding. By being actively involved in the lesson activities (instead of being left out, bored or frustrated) they are less prone to disrupt. The high ability students also benefit through the process of guiding and supporting their fellow group members – their understanding of the material is reinforced.

3. It saves the teacher time. Once students get used to the cooperative learning framework they effectively teach themselves and assist each other. The teacher is free from constant requests for help and attention and can give quality support when it is required rather than when it is demanded.

4. Social skills are naturally developed. Self-expression, decision making, responsibility, accountability, sharing, listening and conflict management are naturally practised and developed during group work sessions. This has the knock-on effect of reducing the occurrence of behaviour problems brought about due to a lack of these skills.

An easy way to group your students into cooperative learning teams

Forming cooperative learning groupings is obviously not as straightforward as having a row of students in alphabetical order but the following simple method will help. All you need is a class list with students ranked according to their ability level and some sticky notes.

To make the process as straightforward as possible, we rank ability by just three broad groups – low, medium and high. You can use a computer spreadsheet to organise the students if your class list is on a database but it's not really necessary. You can use paper or even the back of a beer mat if you're doing this in the pub after work.

Next, using your ability ranked class list, write the name of each student on a colour coded sticky note. The medium ability students will be subdivided into two groups so you will have four groups in total – highs on one colour note, lows on another and the two medium groups on two different coloured notes.

Groups can now be selected by taking one student from each colour group and putting them together on a team sheet (a large piece of paper or card). Individuals can easily be moved from group to group until a satisfactory grouping is obtained, thanks to the wonderful re-stickability properties of the sticky note, and the finished team sheet can then be put on display for easy reference.

Remember that some students just love to mess teachers around by changing the arrangement of the notes to cause confusion. You can prevent that by coating the sheet with some clear polythene/Perspex – or by employing the traditional method of shouting at them.

A note on gender: It may not always be possible to have an equal ratio of boys to girls on each team, but wherever possible be careful if you have one boy with three girls or vice versa. This grouping usually results in the odd one out either being totally ignored or, if the gene pool has been kind to them, being given undue attention. It is better to have two of each gender on as many teams as possible and then, if necessary, have a team all of the same sex for the remainders.

Chapter 9
Getting them into the room – the filter method

Okay, back to the students we left standing outside the door. We'll look at how to deal with any who aren't responding appropriately to you in a moment. For now, though, let's assume that most of your students are compliant and starting to settle down. The next step is to get them into the classroom.

The method we're going to use to get our reasonably well-settled students into the classroom is called the filter method and it goes like this:

The filter method

1. Give the instruction to line up

For the last few minutes you've been gently settling the group down with some non-confrontational reminders and general chit-chat. You now need to move the students from what they essentially view as 'play time' to 'work time' and you do that by changing your positioning (moving away from the students, e.g. to the other side of the corridor) and altering your voice (i.e. tone and volume).

It's time to give one calm, clear, formal instruction to line up:

> Okay, let's make a start. You all need to line up behind (insert student's name) now please, facing this way, without talking.

You could also add a time limit and/or make the instructions more explicit:

> Okay, by the time I reach zero you need to be standing in a line facing the door, with your left shoulder touching the wall in total silence. Five ... four ... three ... two ... one ... zero.

2. Direct your next instruction only at those students who have done as you asked

As we've already discussed, it's far easier dealing with a small group than a large group so in this next step you are going to separate your students into 'listeners' and 'non-listeners'. The idea is that the listeners are clearly more receptive and therefore more likely to follow your next instruction:

> Okay, you people come to the front of the line please. You've done as I asked, thank you. I need to speak to you separately.

And then give them very clear instructions as to what you want them to do next. Something like:

> You're going to go into the room and sit in your *allocated* seat. (You can either have the plan up on the wall or labels on each desk, hand them a chair number on a card as they walk into the room or just point at the chair you want them to sit in.)

> There is a starter activity on the board which you need to get on with in silence. You've shown that you can follow instructions so I'm relying on you to be sensible enough to be in the room on your own. If anyone starts talking or messing around I'll bring you straight back out, okay?

> Right, away you go, and thank you all of you for being so mature.

3. Let them into the room

Let the first group into the room in single file, but be prepared to bring back anyone who runs to their chair, pushes another student, starts shouting and so on. Anyone who behaves like this isn't following your instructions so tell them to come straight out again. At the same time, make a point of acknowledging the students who are behaving appropriately.

> Jonny, come back outside, please. At the moment I'm only letting students enter the classroom who can sit in their seats without pushing, running or shouting. Well done the rest of you. Thank you for doing as I asked.

After going through this process you will be left with the students who either didn't hear your line up instructions the first time or, of course, chose not to.

4. Repeat your instruction to line up

The next step is to repeat the instruction to line up to those students who are still standing with you in the corridor. You will find that a few more will now be ready to line up and enter the room – partly because they have seen the first group of students go in and partly because some of them will have just needed an extra moment or two to register your instructions. You can now repeat steps 2 and 3 with this new group of listeners.

5. Occupy the students in the classroom

You will now be left with a handful (hopefully) of students in the corridor who obviously aren't ready to go into the classroom yet without further input from you. This means you have very effectively filtered out (hence the name of the strategy) most of the potential troublemakers, rather than have them roll into the classroom unhindered and cause a mountain of stress for you to deal with throughout the lesson.

The students you're left with now obviously need a little more attention. Some may need reassurance (e.g. those who often find the work too difficult or who feel uneasy in the presence of other members of the group), some may need cajoling and others need to be calmly reminded of the rules and consequences.

We'll take care of these students in a moment. First, let's make sure that the students that you've just let into the classroom are adequately occupied. This is where settling starter activities come in very handy.

A settling starter activity is a simple task or activity that can be completed independently – a task that students can just get on with without having to ask questions and without needing help or assistance. Clearly, if you hit them with something boring, frustrating, difficult or unappealing in any way whatsoever they are going to either avoid it or need your assistance, and either option is going to take up your attention. You need to give them something simple and engaging.

We'll look at some activity ideas when we come to the start of the lesson in Chapter 10, but right now let me mention one more thing you need to consider – equipment. A good proportion of students in this group are unlikely to bring anything to write with. If you don't pre-empt this you're opening yourself up to yet another time consuming, disruptive setback to sort out. We're all about preventing as many problems as possible, remember, so take the time to provide either a pen/pencil on each desk or a container of them on your desk at the front. (If you need more strategies for dealing with students who routinely neglect to bring equipment to class, see pages 237–239.)

The students who are now in the room have demonstrated that they can follow instructions and have shown that they can be trusted. As long as you have something to occupy them (i.e. the starter work) and as long as you leave the door open and keep popping your head in, you should have a few minutes here to sort out the stragglers at the door.

6. Deal with the students who are still outside in the corridor

This is where the fun starts. The students you're left with in the corridor are those who have deliberately ignored your instructions, so you may be tempted at this stage to lose your temper. ('Okay, the rest of you, I'm going to let you into the room, *but* I'll be watching you like a hawk. If there's *any* messing around at all you'll be out again and in detention. Do I make myself clear?!')

You must be firm at this stage but shouting and making threats aren't the best approach. Treat your most challenging students as you would hope and expect someone would treat your own children and you'll not go far wrong. (If you haven't got children of your own you can substitute your loved one of choice. Or your cat.)

Instead, address a student who doesn't respond appropriately at the door in this way:

> Jonny, much though I want you in the lesson today, I can't let you into the room until I know you are ready to listen and follow instructions. I'm bound by school regulations which state that I must be in full control in the class-room, so if I can't trust you, I can't let you in.

> You're going to have to stay out here in the corridor until you really are ready to follow my instructions and do exactly as I say. Until you do so, you're effectively out of control and it would be against school regulations for me to have you in the room. At this stage, I want you to know you're not in detention or in trouble – I just need to know that you're going to do as I ask, so I'm going to leave you here to have a think about things for a few minutes.

> I'll come back and check on you in three or four minutes and if you're ready to follow my instructions you can come straight in. I'll be back to see what you've decided very soon. Please wait right here.

Note: The success of this last script is almost entirely dependent on the tone you use and your approach. If it sounds as if you're deliberately trying to make life difficult for Jonny, it won't work. At best, you'll get some reluctant compli-ance for a limited time; at worst, if they are pushed too far, the student will simply strop off down the corridor and go AWOL. For that reason, when giving an ultimatum like this, try to use a calm, understanding tone.

If you do manage to keep your emotions in check you can generally expect one of two reactions: Jonny will either promise to behave and ask you to let him in with everyone else (this usually happens in a school where corridors are regularly patrolled by senior staff on the prowl for students who have been sent out of lessons) or, more usually, he will shrug his shoulders and indicate he would rather stay in the corridor.

In both cases the answer is the same – you leave him to think alone in the corridor for a minute or two before you give him any more attention and don't get drawn into an argument with him. Do not under any circumstances give in at this point. After this vital 'think time' you can give him the opportunity to come into the lesson – on your terms.

Teacher: Okay, Jonny, are you ready to come in?

Jonny: I suppose so.

Teacher: That's not good enough, Jonny. I said I needed you to follow instructions 100%, so I'll ask you again. Are you ready to come into the lesson and follow instructions?

Jonny: Yes sir.

Teacher: Great! I'm really pleased. (Remember to smile!) Okay, I've put a desk at the front for you on your own. If you can manage to work there quietly, without causing any problems/talking for ten minutes, I'll let you move to your usual seat with your friends. If you mess around you'll be staying at the front desk. Fair enough?

Jonny: (No answer)

Teacher: Fair enough, Jonny?

Jonny: Yes sir.

Teacher: Great – let's go.

If Jonny still refuses to join the lesson at this stage you could give him some more 'think time' (very important if he is particularly wound up), set up an isolated desk in your classroom for him or, if you feel he is being deliberately quarrelsome, move up through your hierarchy of consequences (see Chapter 4 for more on consequences).

If you're dealing with more than one student at the door, you will need to address them as a group in order to assess whether or not they are sufficiently responsive to be allowed into your classroom. Obviously, it's a good idea to separate non-compliant students as soon as possible and you have a number of options available to you in terms of where to put them. One child can be left in the corridor if necessary – as we did with Jonny in the example above. Providing one or more isolated desks in your room (preferably near your desk at the front) will accommodate two or three more. For students who are proving more difficult to settle you also have the option of 'temporary parking' (see page 28) or removal to a time-out room (depending on school policy).

Note: The process of giving the last few students extra attention shouldn't take more than a couple of minutes – you have a room full of students who need monitoring so you obviously can't afford to spend too long on this.

 You can find a video explaining the filter method at: www. noisyclass.com/bookresources.

Chapter 10
Getting the lesson started

At this point the class has calmed down and you've got them in their seats. If it's a really lively group and you've been using the filter method they will have also been engaged in a settling starter activity (see below). We are now ready to make a proper start to the lesson. The first five minutes of any lesson usually dictate how the lesson will continue and conclude, so it's important to get your lesson started in the right manner.

We're going to cover four different ways you can start a lesson: the formal start, the settled start, the fun start and the engaging question start.

The formal start

The formal start usually commences with administration duties, such as taking the register, before launching into an explanation, demonstration or introductory lesson task of some sort.

Taking a register can actually be a great way to settle and prepare the group for the opening teaching activity, but only if the teacher commands sufficient respect to maintain control throughout the process. If not, it can quickly turn into a circus of silly noises, false names and wind-ups, making for a very chaotic lesson start which is difficult to overcome.

With a tough group, if you have any doubts as to your ability to maintain order, I suggest taking the register on an informal basis – checking names while students are engaged quietly in an appropriate activity such as those explained in the settled start.

The formal start is reserved for reasonably malleable, sensible groups of students with which the teacher commands a suitable amount of respect. If you are struggling with a particular class and find the students aren't responding to you during registration, the settled start offers a more controlled opening to the lesson and works very well with the filter method explained in Chapter 9.

The settled start

The settled start basically involves getting students sat down and engaged in an activity as soon as possible. The aim is to take some of the energy out of a lively group and get them in a frame of mind where they are more receptive to listening and learning.

The settled start is built around one core task – the settling starter activity (for some suggestions see below). I like to call these activities your 'extra pair of hands' because they require no input or support from you once you get them going. As such, they can be used to occupy students for a few moments while you deal with administrative matters or other students who need your attention.

With some groups, particularly those needing and benefiting from total consistency, the settled start should become a routine for the start of every lesson. In this way, the students know exactly what to do as soon as they walk into the room. They put their bags away, choose one of the activities from a list on the board, collect the necessary materials and just get on with it. I normally have some relaxing music quietly playing in the background as they arrive to create a calm and inviting atmosphere.

Since initiating the settled start with difficult groups, I have noticed a huge change in their attitude to lessons. Some of these young people have such chaotic and frenzied lives outside school that they really seem to welcome this quiet time to just relax and settle – it's something they don't get much opportunity to do. And, of course, it gives me a few extra minutes to spend with any students in need of a little extra attention before we get started on the main focus of the lesson.

The type of activity used for settled start is important. It needs to be something sufficiently challenging and engaging to hold their attention, though not confusing enough to require them to ask questions. Remember, you're using this as an extra pair of hands for a few minutes, so it has to be something that is easy for them to get on with minimal teacher input. Choose something simple that requires little verbal explanation or fuss. Each activity should include easy to follow written instructions, if necessary (Step 1: Do this … Step 2: Do this …), as well as a time limit or completion target.

The time limit/target serves a double purpose: it adds weight to a simple activity that might otherwise not be taken seriously and it means you can tailor the same activity to differing ability levels. You would give a more capable student a higher target (e.g. 'You have five minutes to do …' 'You must answer five questions on …') than you would a less capable student or one who arrives late to class.

Some groups/students will respond very well to being given a choice of activities – choice being a powerful motivator – so you might want to try having several drawers/bins/trays of ready-made settling starter activities on offer from which students can select their preferred activity. However, this can also cause disruption when, having chosen an activity and then decided he doesn't like it, Jonny spends the next ten minutes leafing through all the other activities on offer instead of actually getting down to work. In this case, choice becomes a handy avoidance tactic. I have used both approaches with different groups – it works with some and not with others, so the choice is yours.

If your settling starter activity is to copy notes from the board or a book, make sure there isn't a huge amount of text otherwise it will provoke complaints. Some students will take one look at a large block of text and it will cause panic (and probably a torrent of abuse). You can 'hide' extra work if this is the case by having five or ten lines of text for them to copy and then have a note at the end saying, 'Now answer question 2 on page 46' which could be another five or ten lines of notes.

Add the following sentence as a written or verbal instruction when you issue any settling starter activity: 'You have ____ minutes to complete the task. If it isn't completed in this time you will have to finish it at break/after school.'

If a student doesn't finish this activity they must do it in their own time – they finish it at breaktime or they come back at the end of school and do it then. This needs to be followed up with *every* miscreant *every* time because they need to see that if they don't do this activity in the allotted time then they will have to face consequences.

Even if they have to take the work home, it must get done. The upshot for you if you don't follow up is that they see the activity as a waste of time and are therefore less likely to do a similar activity (or any activity for that matter) in future. With this in mind, don't make your settling starter activities too taxing or they will backfire. Their purpose is to settle students down, not wind them up!

Suggested settling starter activities

The following generic activities all work as settling starters, depending on the subject/topic:

- Copying short sections of text from a book (for some unknown reason my students love reproducing passages of writing).

- Drawing and labelling a diagram.

- Practising filling in 'real life' forms (e.g. application forms for driving licences, passports).

- Word searches and puzzles.

- Hobby or topic work – for example, producing a booklet about their favourite subject.

- Silent reading (obviously choose books they actually enjoy reading).

- Producing a poster.

- Colouring (it's amazing how relaxing and absorbing it can be to simply colour in an outline drawing carefully – very Zen!).

- Writing a diary/journal entry.

- Cloze activities.

- Treasure hunt or comprehension activities – for example, retrieving information from given sources.

- Watching a video – give each student a sheet with simple comprehension questions about the video clip as it helps keep them focused.

- 'Getting to know you' activities – these are one of my favourites because as well as occupying students, you get to learn all about their likes/dislikes, passions and hobbies, and this information is crucial for having conversations and building relationships with them.

Alternatively, you could use a ready-made activity like the two listed below.

Odd one out

Materials: None required, but some thought needs to go into the groups of words chosen.

Time: 5–10 minutes

Overview: Triplets of subject related key words are written on the board or issued to students on entry to the classroom and students must decide which is the odd one out.

Directions:

1. Write three or four triplets of key words on the board, a worksheet or postcard (e.g. farming, drilling for oil, hairdressing; Pacific, Atlantic, Asia; hospital, block of flats, cinema).

2. The students must identify the odd one out and give a reason for their choice. There is no 'right' or 'wrong' in this exercise – as long as students can give explanations which are logical and/or convincingly explained their answer should be acceptable. The idea is to develop thinking and communication skills.

 ## Crack the code

Materials: Pen, paper and envelope containing the secret code key and a key word list for each student.

Time: 5–10 minutes

Overview: A creative thinking starter which can be adapted to suit most subjects and topics.

Directions:

1. Develop a secret code alphabet consisting of a symbol or image for each letter of the alphabet. Give each student a copy, together with a list of key words about the lesson, in an envelope (label it 'Spy Kit' or 'Mission Documents') as they enter the room (or place it on their desks).

2. Write a message on the board relating to the lesson using symbols from your coded alphabet – for example, 'Today you will learn about (key word/topic focus)'.

3. Ask the students to decode the message and write their key word list in a coded form. More able students can be given longer key word lists.

4. Students can also trade papers to decode each other's messages.

5. The same activity can be used as a plenary by asking students to write what they learned during the lesson in code.

Okay, that's enough fun, let's get back to the task in hand: settling the students.

With a very challenging, energetic group it may be prudent (or necessary) to continue with the settling process you started outside the door – perhaps chatting with table groups, making positive statements and being quick to praise those who are doing as you have asked.

The settled start should run for no more than ten minutes at most, depending on the group. From here, you need to make the transition to the next activity which will normally be a 'proper' teaching and learning task. Transition time can create an element of disruption with any group but with a challenging class it can become total mayhem unless it is pre-planned and well-managed.

When you feel the students are ready to move to your main teaching activity give them a 30 second warning ('We'll be stopping this activity in 30 seconds so start thinking about finishing whatever you're doing and packing away ready for the next instructions'). The reason for the warning is simple: if your students are engrossed in a nice activity or a quiet conversation, the instruction to pack up will take more than a few seconds to register. By giving them an advance warning you reduce the need to start nagging them to hurry up.

Once the students have stopped work and are attentive, give clear step-by-step instructions to pack away their materials/equipment, if necessary, and be ready for the main teaching task. The students should now be in a state where they are much more likely to do some work.

Before giving any detailed instructions to a group of students in class, make sure they are all completely silent and giving you eye contact. If you don't instil this as a habit and insist on this level of attention, your students will not take you seriously. I can't emphasise this enough – this is *your* classroom and *you* are in charge. But you can only be in charge if the students actually listen to you.

The fun start

The third start is to grab the attention of the entire group by starting the lesson with a bang. This is my preferred way to start a lesson – but there is a caveat here. The danger you face with high energy activities is that some groups can get far too silly and are then reluctant (or too hyped up) to work on other tasks afterwards.

So the fun start should be used with caution. If you don't feel confident in regaining control of the group when they are engaged in lively activities then this is not a good option for you, certainly not at first. If you've tried a fun activity with another, easier group and it went well, maybe you could try the same activity with a tougher group, but if you think you're going to struggle use one of the other lesson starts. Once you have a little more control over the group you can then start to have more fun with them.

So what happens during the fun start? This is where we use amusing, exciting and often energetic activities which young people enjoy. Fun starter activities can be curriculum related but non-academic starters are also useful to gain the attention of a group with entrenched negativity towards learning. Once a tough group starts to experience some positive emotions in a lesson (fun being one of them), their whole attitude to you and to your subject will change – and quickly. Here's an example.

What's in the bag?

Materials: Prop related to the lesson content together with a suitable bag or container.

Time: 10 minutes

Overview: A subject related prop is hidden in a bag or container (if possible, try to find a container which naturally generates a level of intrigue or excitement – so avoid carrier bags from Lidl) and the students have to guess what is inside. Younger students may enjoy this as a regular routine ('What's in the bag today?') but older students also enjoy it as an occasional warm-up.

Directions:

1.   Write on the board: 'You have 20 chances to guess what's in the bag.'

2.   Explain to students that they can volunteer to ask a question to try to determine what's in the bag. Questions can only be those which have a 'yes' or 'no' answer (i.e. they can ask 'Is it blue?' but not 'What colour is it?').

3.   Write their questions on the board one at a time to keep track of the total number asked and to avoid repeated questions. Answer them 'yes' or 'no' and put a tick or a cross next to the question. (I always like to have two noise effects for right and wrong answers to add to the humorous atmosphere – a kazoo or duck call for wrong answers and a bugle horn or quiz master's bell for right answers. Be sure to carry an even-tempered duck if you choose this route.)

4.   Tension mounts once their questions are into double figures as they realise they might not succeed – particularly when you tell them they will get extra homework if they don't get the right answer!

More fun starters are available at the online resource which accompanies this book: www.noisyclass.com/bookresources.

The engaging question start

The engaging question start is a near foolproof way of getting a challenging group of students involved at the start of the lesson. It relies on asking questions which they find highly relevant to their lives.

Like many teachers, I used to start the majority of my lessons with a question relating to the topic focus. For example, if I was doing a lesson on the circulatory system, my opening question might be, 'How many of you can explain what a blood vessel is?' A few students would be eager to answer me and their hands would shoot up so I thought I was doing the right thing – I had some participation after all. But for every hand that went up there were ten more that didn't. A significant proportion of the students simply weren't taking part. And if they aren't taking part, as we well know, they soon start to misbehave.

Let's face it, it was a dull question. No matter how passionately it is delivered that type of question isn't likely to generate much involvement from the group. Questions like this rely on volunteers, and if you rely on volunteers you are immediately switching your attention and lesson focus towards those students who already want to learn.

That makes it far too easy for those who aren't motivated to learn to simply sit and watch, perhaps pretending to listen. Why should they bother taking part? They find the subject dull and they either don't know the answer to the question or just don't want to answer. Maybe they are afraid of looking swotty in front of their friends, or maybe they just don't want to risk the embarrassment of getting it wrong. It's easier just to sit and watch. Or sit and fiddle. Or mess about.

If you want to get the non-volunteers involved you've got to have a question they can relate to – something that connects with their interests or is at least relevant to their lives and experiences. Why would they even care how blood gets around the body unless the question is applicable to them?

We'll look at some different ways of making your lessons more relevant to students later in Chapter 11 but for now, see if you can spot the engaging questions in the following sets:

1. Who can tell me how blood gets around the body?

2. Who knows what a blood vessel is?

3. Can anyone tell me what a blood capillary is?

4. Have you ever accidentally cut yourself?

1. What do you think is going through Macbeth's mind after he kills Duncan?

2. How does Macbeth's character change after he kills Duncan?

3. What words would you use to describe Macbeth at the start of the play?

4. When was the last time you did something really terrible that you later regretted?

Can you see why a group of disengaged students would be most likely to respond to (4) in both cases? These questions hook them in by giving them an opportunity to think about events that are applicable to them. They appeal to the students because they present an opportunity to share their experiences.

Once your students are animated and actively taking part – no doubt by sharing tales of bleeding limbs – *then* you can lead them into the lesson content.

So, going back to our lesson on circulation, we could go on to ask:

- How long did it bleed for?

- How did you stop the bleeding?

- Do you think it would have stopped if you had just left it?

And then, finally, we can lead the students on to the main content of the lesson:

- Where does the blood come from, and how does it get to the cut?

Hopefully you can see that the engaging question start provides a reliable means of hooking your students in and getting them involved. The key is relevancy, so in the next chapter we'll look at some additional ways to use relevancy to make lessons more engaging.

Chapter 11
Maintaining a positive learning environment

Okay, let's quickly recap. We've settled the students outside the room using non-confrontational reminders and informal chit-chat so that they are more likely to follow our instructions. We've then got them into the room under control (using the filter method for extremely lively groups) and we've made a successful opening to the lesson using one of our four main types of lesson starter.

We'll come on to later how we deal with any students who aren't settled at this stage, those who drift off task plus a wide range of other disruptions, but what we need to do now is maintain this calm, productive learning environment for the students who are currently engaged. In this chapter we'll go through some general suggestions for keeping the lesson flowing as well as some ideas for making lessons more interesting.

Engaging lessons

When faced with a disruptive class over a long period, some teachers tend to stop trying hard to engage the class (which is understandable) and instead resort to dull, uninspiring lesson tasks. While the occasional copying from the board or worksheet based lesson is fine to remind them what they are missing, or to give yourself a well-earned break, if these tedious activities become the norm, then behaviour will undoubtedly deteriorate.

Some years ago I had an experience which made me appreciate the huge importance of engaging learning activities in terms of preventing behaviour problems in class. I was working in a pupil referral unit where every minute of every day was spent focusing on addressing bad behaviour. From 8.30 a.m. until 3.30 p.m. the attention of every member of staff was firmly focused on trying to help the students get through the day without either causing or being involved in a serious incident. It was very tiring and stressful.

On this particular day we were instructed by the head to take our respective class members to the hall as there was to be an interactive lesson provided by a company working with reptiles, large insects and assorted creepy-crawlies from far off countries. The usual response from the students to any outside agency was at best rude and at worst quite violent so I approached the hall with some trepidation.

And then a strange thing happened. As the students entered the hall, the young woman in charge of the animals stood at the door to greet them warmly with a smile. She held one finger to her lips gesturing 'please be quiet'. In her other hand, close to her chest, she held a rat. Behind her were about eight crates and boxes with lids on. Some of them were semi-transparent and you could just make out something moving around jerkily within. One of the boxes had a very large, hairy insect leg protruding from under the lid.

The effect on the behaviour of our students was miraculous. Their whole demeanour changed as soon as they entered the room. They slowed down, their eyes widened and they moved towards the rows of seats in silence. Once everyone was in the room, the young woman introduced herself and proceeded to talk about each of the animals in turn. She allowed those who wanted to the chance to stroke them and examine them more closely.

Only moments earlier several of these kids had been fighting viciously. These teenagers were frequently found on the roof of the building throwing stones or screaming abuse at staff. And yet here they were sitting engrossed in a learning activity. They were absolutely transfixed, and I realised that for the very first time not one member of staff was having to deal with a behaviour related issue.

Now, don't get me wrong. I realise we can't produce a box of snakes and tarantulas every time we are presented with a difficult group, but we can learn from this experience. If you provide students with an activity which interests and engages them, you will have less to do in terms of managing behaviour.

So how do *you* do that? How do you make *your* lessons more successful and more appealing to students when the lady with the hairy legs isn't available?

The secret to making your lessons more appealing and engaging

I like to use an analogy which simplifies the task of engaging students considerably – I call it the 'emotion rucksack'. If you're faced with students dragging their heels and groaning as they walk up the corridor towards your classroom, it's obvious they have already made up their minds that the lesson is going to be something they have to endure rather than something they will actually enjoy.

In this situation, I imagine these students each carrying a huge rucksack on their back filled with undesirable emotions. They are weighed down with negative thoughts, feelings and emotions about a particular lesson (and probably about school and life in general). These thoughts, feelings and emotions are often based on their personal past experiences – previous lessons they have attended or perhaps just comments from peers ('I hate that lesson and you should too').

Let's say, for example, that in one or more previous lessons they have struggled to grasp the skills required to complete the assigned work tasks. If that's the case, they will almost certainly be bringing a degree of frustration, anxiety and perhaps fear and inadequacy in their rucksack to the next lesson. If they feel they have been picked on by the teacher in previous lessons, they will be carrying feelings of distrust and perhaps even anger or revenge. If they found the subject too simple, completely boring or totally irrelevant, they will likely be carrying annoyance, irritation or apathy.

I'm sure you get the idea. Most, if not all, challenging students are arriving at the classroom door having already decided that the lesson is something they are not going to enjoy or benefit from. And it is very difficult to teach them and manage their behaviour when they are in this state.

The way around this problem is actually very simple. All you have to do is change what they are carrying in their rucksack. If we can have our students walking into class carrying a little bit of intrigue because of an interesting demonstration or story we shared last lesson, or optimism based on the (appropriate) fun and laughter they experienced last lesson, they are likely to be more enthusiastic about returning to class.

If they are carrying recollections of a brief taste of success and achievement they felt having understood a difficult concept for the first time, or feelings of confidence based on the praise they received for their efforts, or a sense of camaraderie or acceptance as the result of a successful group work session, we can expect them to be happy to return to class and to be in a state more conducive to learning when they do so.

What you want is students coming to your lessons looking forward to learning and being with you because they enjoyed your lesson. If they succeeded, achieved, discovered, learned something interesting, had fun, shared a laugh, improved and felt better about themselves; if they were motivated, cared for and moved emotionally, it stands to reason that they will feel more optimistic about the next lesson because they can expect more of the same.

These are things that any teacher can put in place in any lesson. It comes down to helping the students to feel wanted, valued and appreciated and making sure that they gain something positive from the short period of time you spend together.

Ten ways to make lessons appealing and engaging

1. Use lots of genuine praise

When negative behaviour has become entrenched (as it does with a very difficult group), we tend to focus on what is going wrong in the classroom ('I told you to be quiet!''That's the third time I've had to tell you!''Be quiet!'). And this makes for a very negative environment, reinforcing the group's entrenched view that school is not a particularly nice place to be.

Focusing on what the students are doing right seems counter-intuitive (they need to be told, dammit!) but it is the quickest way I know of to transform negative moods. I don't care what anyone says: there is not a child on the planet who, deep down, doesn't want to succeed. And if you are the (only) one who consistently recognises and acknowledges when they have tried to do something right or made an effort – no matter how small – to improve, they *will* respond to you. The only caveat is that praise must only be given at the right time (i.e. when it is deserved) and in the right way. (For more on praise see Chapter 6.)

2. Make sure the tasks are achievable and appropriate

The joy of achievement is something which tough students rarely experience in school. They seldom get to enjoy the personal feelings of satisfaction associated with working hard at a task and seeing it through to completion. And yet mastery in a subject is widely cited as one of the most powerful motivators, so we must strive to give our toughest students maximum opportunity to feel competent, to achieve and to succeed if we are to encourage them to attempt future work tasks and to raise their enthusiasm for learning.

Often these students are reluctant to go to class purely because they are so used to failing (and continually being criticised for doing so). Their fear of looking foolish and their unwillingness to try is often masked by inappropriate or silly behaviour and other avoidance tactics. One of the lecturers on my PGCE teacher training course many years ago had an impressive way of highlighting the importance of this.

At the start of an afternoon lecture session towards the end of the course, Mr A (as he was affectionately known) announced proudly that the class was to be privy to a revolutionary new standardised science test that a private company would be marketing to schools in the near future. He thought it would be a wonderful addition to our training if we were to spend half an hour or so piloting it during our next session – with us acting the part of school students. He had managed to get the company to agree to the trial.

He explained that we would be required to adhere to strict exam conditions and when we returned the next day the furniture had already been rearranged in rows. We were directed to our places and sat in silence awaiting the test papers. While we were waiting he introduced a very stern woman wearing a smart business suit. She wore a badge indicating she represented Star Education – the company that was marketing the new tests. After a brief introduction, and satisfied that we understood the serious nature of the pilot and the importance of attempting all the questions, she indicated that the papers could be given out.

Nothing could have prepared me for that test. I'm not naturally the calmest of people in challenging situations and I must admit I had always found exams at school very stressful. But that was nothing to how I felt when I began to read the questions on this paper! I honestly couldn't make one iota of sense of them. My mind was twisting, my palms were sweaty and my heart was racing – I was really struggling.

I looked round the room and was relieved to see other people clearly having as much difficulty as I was. A few individuals were scribbling furiously but you could tell they were in a panic, jotting an answer down then scrubbing it out and trying another possible solution. By the expressions on their faces, their new solution didn't work either.

Remembering my old school days, I did what I always did at the start of a test when I realised I didn't have a hope in hell of coming up with an answer to the first question – I skimmed over the rest of them, hoping to find a lifeline, that one gleaming pearl I understood and could at least attempt. But there wasn't one question on the paper I had a hope of answering confidently.

I started to make my frustrations heard. I pushed the paper away, slammed my pencil down and muttered an obscenity. Someone behind me sniggered. A piece of crumpled paper – a test paper – was thrown from the back of the room. Clearly someone else had also given up. And then suddenly the room erupted. A few people remained silent and did their best to complete the test but the majority of us were seething. We were incensed at having been given such a ridiculously incomprehensible task. Hands went up. A young woman stormed out of the room dismissively shaking her head at the frowning adjudicator. Her cry of, 'This is f****** stupid!' summed up everyone's frustration.

In response to the pandemonium, both our lecturer and the stern woman in charge of the test slowly made their way to the front of the room and turned to face us. The room fell silent. We waited for Mr A to tell us what would happen next. 'Well, thank you everyone for so willingly taking part in the pilot, and may I take this opportunity to introduce you to my wife.' He gestured to the woman beside him. 'She doesn't really work for Star Education. There is no such company to my knowledge; we made the test up a couple of days ago.' He paused, a smile creeping onto his face, before continuing, 'Now you know what it feels like to be a child who is given work that is far too difficult for them!'

What always amazes me when I think about this incident is that every single person in the room that day was an adult and a professional – we were just days away from being qualified as teachers. And yet our behaviour was that of maladjusted teenagers. All the frustrating behaviours we complain about in the classroom were on display – muttering obscenities, throwing equipment around the room, shouting, talking out of turn, leaving the room without permission, arguing with the teacher – and it was due solely to the work task being too difficult and too confusing.

Colleagues I've shared this with tell me they often think of that story when planning any kind of activity, particularly for children with special educational needs, and are reminded of it whenever a lesson fails miserably. It highlights the extreme importance of making sure that work tasks are both achievable and appropriate. If the work is too easy students will get bored – and will tell you so. If it's too difficult you will encounter mayhem.

 ## Three simple ways to make sure work tasks don't overwhelm students and cause disruption

1. Pitch work at their ability level.

2. Avoid work that is text heavy.

3. Don't feed them all at once – split work into bite sized chunks.

Particularly when working with pupils with emotional and behavioural difficulties, it pays to break tasks up into small chunks. This is particularly necessary when you have to complete assessments with difficult children. There is nothing wrong with breaking a test up into a series of smaller tests and giving them to pupils over a series of days rather than in one very stressful session. As long as the work gets done, where's the problem? Similarly, if you sense that a student is struggling with the work you've set them, take some of it away or cover it up – let them focus on an amount that they feel is achievable.

Always bear in mind that those students who show reluctance to take part in an activity, or are intent on disrupting your lessons to avoid working, may well be doing so because of a fear of failure.

3. Use music and sound effects

Music has a massive effect on young people – it is such a vital and influential part of their lives that we must include it somehow. You can use it to relax your students and focus their attention or to enhance creativity and boost achievement. Music can energise and bring new life to a tired group, just as it can calm down a hyped-up individual. It can provide fun and a change of mindset as well as building rapport and encouraging bonding. The right music, in the right situation, is a great team builder and a valuable aid to learning. And, of course, the opportunity to laugh at teacher's gramophone record collection is always welcome.

Similarly, sound effects can be used in a variety of ways in the classroom. From rapturous game show applause when students answer questions correctly to the sound of a machine gun when they are being cheeky, sound effects can bring laughter to a lesson. Mobile technology makes this easy and accessible. Most mobile phones can be plugged into a speaker system and then used to access all manner of sound effect applications, and it's amazing just how realistic these are. Just for kicks, I often use my iPhone to trick the kids outside our house into thinking the ice cream van has arrived.

Four ways to use music in the classroom

1. Use music to set the mood and mark transitions

Different types of music can be played at appropriate times during a lesson to motivate, calm, focus or relax students, with different tempos and genres being more suited to particular types of activity. A CD of TV and film theme tunes is a great investment for this. You could play 'Welcome to the Jungle' as the students arrive, the title theme from *Chariots of Fire*, the *Rocky* title track 'Gonna Fly Now' or the 'Theme from *Mission: Impossible*' during tough tasks, *The Benny Hill Show* theme tune when you want them to change activities or the *Countdown* clock music when you want them to answer spot questions.

Music also provides an aid to marking transitions between different lesson activities. Slowly turning the track off once all the students are at their desks gives a clear indication that the lesson is about to formally start and is far less abrasive than the usual, 'Quiet! Let's make a start!'

A session of active learning, in which students are expected and encouraged to be moving freely around the room, could be accompanied by some lively dance music to keep the pace going, while a discussion would favour a slower, less intrusive tempo. Playing this new track at a lower volume would promote a more settled atmosphere while still providing some cover for those who are reluctant to speak out. It can be daunting for self-conscious students to have their say during discussions. Another tune could be brought in towards the end of the debate to signify the transition to the next activity or to bring the lesson to a close. At the end, some uplifting music would help to cement positive emotions as the students file out of the room – the title theme from *The Great Escape* perhaps.

Baroque music has been found to stimulate right-side brain activity and aid concentration, and can be an excellent accompaniment to small group discussions and cooperative work or as calming background music as your students enter the room.

2. Use music to settle and harmonise the class

Classical music can have a surprisingly positive effect on the classroom environment. Some of the most challenging pupils I have taught complained bitterly when I first introduced classics such as Ravel's *Boléro* as background music to our lessons, swearing that the only sound they could possibly listen to was hardcore house. At first, predictably, we got nowhere – they would actually sit staring at me with fingers in ears saying repeatedly, 'We're not listenin', it's crap!'

Gradually, as they began to recognise melodies from various adverts and films, they became more tolerant and eventually started asking for certain pieces to be replayed. 'O Fortuna' from Carl Orff's *Carmina Burana* (used in the Old Spice adverts) and Delibes' 'Flower Duet' from the opera *Lakmé* (used by British Airways) were both very popular, but so were many more. The response was actually quite amazing. Although I can provide no hard data to back this up, I believe there was a much calmer atmosphere and a marked decrease in behaviour problems when these pieces of music were played at a moderate volume throughout my lessons.

3. Use music as a classroom management tool

Music can act as a noise screen, masking out unwanted noises and dominant voices which would otherwise distract some workers. In addition, it can provide teachers with necessary privacy when giving feedback to individual learners or when challenging those who aren't participating as they should be.

4. Use music for impromptu furniture repairs

A stack of One Direction CDs is ideal for propping up a wonky table leg.

4. Use props

A prop box full of silly hats, masks, clothes, wigs and jokes is a fun classroom must-have for role play and other activities. Use the props whenever you're introducing a relevant topic or perhaps for the students to wear for recall activities ('Today you must answer the question in the style of a rock star/farmer/airline pilot/weather girl/newsreader, etc. and wear this crazy wig/hat/mask while doing so').

You could wear huge plastic ears or over-sized pink fluffy ear muffs when noise levels get too high; a big inflatable hammer, policeman's helmet, huge vampire fangs or enormous foam boxing gloves can help to take care of students who are just starting to go off the boil; a big roving reporter's microphone is a much better way to ask for answers than hands up; a 'honk-honk' bicycle horn can signify the end of activities; and a Stetson, sheriff's badge or toy pistols can be used to deal with students who get answers wrong in quizzes. Use your imagination!

Subject related props also offer a wonderful way to introduce a new topic. Without doubt the best prop I ever had the privilege to use in a lesson was a genuine relic from the *Titanic*. It was a broken pocket watch belonging to a young boy who had been working as a bellboy on one of the lifts. My students had been working on their research project for a few weeks and were fascinated by the whole *Titanic* story. To see this piece of living history up close and tangible, after previously only having had access to pictures, videos and reference books, was simply amazing for them. They had already discovered the exact time the ship was documented as taking her final plunge, 2.20 a.m., and had filled this time in as the last entry on their timelines. When they saw that the watch had actually stopped at precisely 2.20 a.m. they were, understandably, completely spellbound.

Obviously this was a one-off. The chances of getting your hands on priceless relics are slim and any efforts to procure them from your local museum may not be viewed favourably. I was lucky – not because I had originally arranged to bring in Kate Winslet, but because a friend of mine knew the woman who owned the watch. She had never shown the pocket watch to anyone outside her home up until that point but she was thrilled to be able to enhance the children's education by coming into school to show them. Like I say, I was lucky, but we all have friends and relatives and it's possible that one of them has, or knows someone who has, a suitable prop for your next lesson.

As an introduction to a lesson they can grab attention like nothing else. The *Titanic* watch, for example, was actually introduced to the group as part of a simple fun starter activity, 'What's in the bag?' (see page 162). When the students entered the room, the bag (one of the original sacks used by the authorities to hold passengers' belongings retrieved after the accident) was waiting ominously on the centre table.

5. Include challenge

Someone once told me there are two sure-fire ways to get disinterested students engaged – bet them or pay them. I don't want you to be out of pocket so let's look at the first one. Challenge is a universal motivator but to use it effectively we have to get both the context and the level of challenge right. In terms of context, the challenge has to interest the students. A physical activity will appeal more to physical students, a sports challenge will appeal more to sporty students and a technical challenge will appeal more to geeks (ahem). Finding the right context to motivate disengaged students requires getting to know them so that you can base the challenge on something which interests them.

Setting challenges at the right level is also important. If the challenge is too easy there will be no feeling of success if it is completed, and the student will likely deem it too boring or childish to bother with in the first place. If it is too difficult they will be put off from trying in future challenges.

 ## Quick ways to get challenge into your lessons

- Tell them they can set the maximum number of mistakes they are each allowed in a piece of work.

- Let them choose the question they should answer in a specified time.

- Challenge them to beat your previous class (e.g. 'They managed to be sitting in their seats with their mouths closed and their books open in 7.5 seconds!').

- Use challenges from other people (e.g. 'People looking at your past scores will assume you're going to get a C in this next test. How about we put a plan together to prove them wrong?' 'In the staff meeting this morning all the staff were told that not one class has achieved 100% attendance for a whole term. How about we work together to prove them all wrong?').

- Set a silent challenge – get a timer and build up the time they can stay silent. Start with two or three minutes of silent working, then five, then seven … You'll be surprised how long they can go once they start to experience some success and actually start seeing the benefits of silence.

- Set some fun challenges (e.g. 'I'm betting there isn't a person in this room who can eat four dried crackers in under one minute!'). My favourite A-level biology teacher (I hope you're reading this Mr Finlinson!) set that last challenge to us one day at the start of a module on digestion to illustrate the fact that the breakdown of food starts in the mouth with the action of saliva and chewing. It was messy, and I still smile when I think about it almost 30 years later!

6. Give them some choice

Being given some choice in what they do gives students a sense of control and autonomy, and this moves them from feeling stuck or trapped into action. It gives them a sense of freedom. The simplest way to offer choice is to take some of the pressure out of our requests in order to create more willingness in students to take part.

For example, on test papers the questions which give a choice ('Answer two from section A, two from section B, and two from section C') are less threatening and more appealing than those which offer no choice at all. Instead of, 'Turn to page 20 and get on with the exercises; when you've finished those you can complete this worksheet', try, 'I've written some choices on the board. You only have to do five from the ten choices, and you can do them in any order you like.'

This small difference in the way the work is presented makes a world of difference to the way students respond. Alternatively, you could give the entire class a limited choice in the form of a voting slip (verbal discussion can sometimes lead to arguments and, besides, a vote is more fun) written out as follows.

Which of the following tasks would you prefer?

1.   Produce a mind-map on ...
2.   Produce a newspaper report on ...
3.   Work as a group to find a solution to ...
4.   Complete exercise 5 in the textbook ...

The activity with the most votes wins and by taking part in this vote you agree to take part in the chosen activity without argument.

7. Make work relevant to them

As we saw in Chapter 10, students respond most positively in lessons when tasks and challenges are connected to what they know in the real world. We have to introduce new topics and information to them in a way that is relevant to them if we want them to be interested.

Let me give you an example from my own teaching experience to illustrate how this might be done. I used to teach Shakespeare to teenage boys who had been excluded from mainstream school. These boys seldom spoke in recognisable, grammatically correct sentences – monosyllabic grunts were the chosen mode of expression – so you can probably imagine what they thought of Shakespeare!

The first year I struggled to find suitable resources to engage them. Textbooks that claimed to be packed with engaging activities for low ability, disengaged students proved to be of little use. The government frameworks which provided very prescriptive three-part lessons (written by highly paid consultants) were even less useful. After three or four lessons the mere mention of the word 'Shakespeare' set these boys into a rage, with them threatening to literally rip the room apart if I tried to inflict any more on them.

So how does a teacher introduce a playwright such as Shakespeare, so far removed from modern life, to a group of disaffected 15-year-old boys? How do we get them to identify with Shakespeare as a writer and see him as having something relevant to offer, so that they might be interested enough to at least listen to part of a play – you know, just in case he's actually any good?

My new cohort of students came to my lessons already hating Shakespeare. They hated the language (largely because they couldn't understand it) and other kids in school who had already had to endure him told them that the Shakespeare lessons were, in a word, 'crap'. I was beaten before the lesson had started. They had already made up their minds that Shakespeare was spelled 's**t'.

Yet in the late 1500s and early 1600s, long before the first teenage boys stalked the earth, Shakespeare wrote drama which captured hearts and minds. His plays were tremendously entertaining and the public flocked to see them. He was the Quentin Tarantino of his day (although probably a better actor). So that's how I introduced him to the class. I didn't even mention the name at first. Instead we talked about films the students had all watched. Horror films, comedies and gangster films, such as *Reservoir Dogs*, got them talking. We talked about the emotions they evoked and why they found them so entertaining.

I asked them what they would do without television and cinema. What entertainment was on offer before this technology became such a big part of our lives? Most of them had heard of these buildings called 'theatres' but probably couldn't have told one apart from a supermarket, and none had actually been inside one. So I organised a trip. They loved it. They wanted to know more about this interactive, wonderful form of entertainment. And from that point on they had an interest in William Shakespeare, where previously there had been ignorance, fear and loathing.

Shakespeare was made interesting to these boys over a series of lessons, but the key was first getting them to see that the entertainment they loved was the very same entertainment that was loved hundreds of years ago. It was made relevant to them. Shakespeare wrote comedies and bloody tragedies which were adored by his fans – the film-goers of yesteryear. Once the students could see that there were parallels between the entertainment back then and the blockbusters of today, they were interested to learn more.

 Five ways to make work relevant to your students

1. Link to current real world problems

The integration of the current social context into a subject encourages students to move away from seeing the learning as far removed from their lives. Could you start the lesson by talking about a recent news item (and showing them the story in a newspaper) or a relevant current real life issue that this particular age group are interested in or affected by?

2. Link to their environment

By taking the curriculum out into the real world and showing how knowledge can be used in their own environment we give the learning immediate relevance. Could you start the lesson by linking content to a photograph of their town centre, a newspaper article about their neighbourhood, a news video about a local event or even by taking them out into the community?

3. Link to their interests

In Chapter 5 on building relationships, we looked at the importance of discovering and getting to know your students' interests and hobbies. Linking content to young people's interests is one of the best ways for them to see the importance of a topic, but even in the absence of detailed personal information about each student there are common areas which will be of interest to most – for example, sport, fashion, celebrities, music, gore/horror, any current Xbox/PS4 game, recent blockbuster films and popular TV shows or a place they all congregate at night (local park/mall).

4. Link to age appropriate real life issues

Adolescence can be a very troubling time, with most teenagers encountering issues which they find confusing and difficult. When learning is linked to topics which the students may be experiencing first hand, such as gangs/gang culture, drugs/alcohol, self-confidence and low self-esteem, they are more likely to empathise and therefore more able to see the relevance of what is being presented.

5. Use metaphors and analogies

Metaphors and analogies are one of the very best ways of making new concepts relevant to students because they draw parallels between the new information and previously known, commonplace or everyday objects, happenings or actions. I use metaphors and analogies a lot in my teaching to describe processes, actions and concepts – virtually anything, in fact – because they give students an easy way to grasp and understand new material. You could say it's like turning a light on for them or providing them with a map. Get it?

There is an easy way to come up with a metaphor for virtually anything you're teaching. Just ask yourself a simple question, 'What is it like?' and pick the answer which you feel would be most relevant to your students. For example, diffusion (the spread of particles from regions of higher concentration to regions of lower concentration) is a difficult concept to explain to students, so let's ask the question: 'What is it like?'

1. It's like watching people travelling down a tightly packed escalator and then all spreading out in different directions when they get to the bottom.

2. It's like watching the smoke from a bonfire spread out.

3. It's like hearing a student breaking wind at the back of the class and then watching the succession of other class members clutching their noses as the chemical weapon spreads through the room.

Any one of those analogies could be used to describe the process of diffusion in a way that students who had no concept of the process could relate to; but for some reason, most of my students find analogy (3) easiest to understand.

8. Add a touch of magic

There are some teachers reading this (you may be one of them) who will think the idea of using magic is ridiculous. But magic is amazingly effective for capturing the attention and imagination of your students, for changing the mood of a negative group and also as a 'brain break'. In some cases, tricks can even be adapted to illustrate key points in the curriculum.

I stumbled on the idea of using magic quite by accident. I first started using magic in lessons as a result of a unit of work I was doing with my class on Shakespeare. We had been studying *Macbeth* and their interest in the witches led to discussions on the paranormal, which naturally led to a lesson on magic and illusions – and they enjoyed it tremendously. As a treat, I decided to show them a few simple tricks I had learned from a friend who ran a corporate entertainment business, and the response was just amazing. I couldn't believe how much interest was generated from these simple tricks and illusions, so I tried to show them at least one new trick each week from then on. In time students were bringing in their own tricks to show the rest of the class and it became something of a ritual to have a (excuse the pun) 'magic moment' each week.

I've found that students of all ages love 'mind magic' tricks in which you apparently read their mind or foretell events yet to come. Obviously, you don't actually need to be psychic in order to do these types of tricks – you just need the instructions I've provided below.

Magic trick #1: other people in school

The illusion: Hand out three slips of paper and ask for three student volunteers to help you. Two are asked to write the name of a student in the class on their slip. The third person is asked to write the name of a student from another class/year group.

The three slips are folded and placed in a hat (without you touching them). You are then blindfolded or the hat is held high over your head so you can't see into it. You are able to reach in and bring out the slip of paper with the name of the person from another class written on it. You can adapt this trick to the curriculum by having students choose key words, dates and so on instead.

How it's done: This is a very easy trick. Take a sheet of note paper and tear it into three pieces. The top and bottom pieces will have one smooth edge and one rough edge, but the centre piece will have two rough edges.

Make sure the person who is writing the name of the student from another class writes on the centre slip, while the other two students write down the names of a student in their own class. Get them to fold the slips and drop them into the hat.

When you reach into the hat, all you need to do is feel for the slip with two rough edges. When you have found it, don't bring it out right away. Ask the students to concentrate on the names they have written. Bring out the slip, still folded, and hold it against your head. Build up the suspense until you have created a mystery. Then reveal the slip in your hand as the one with the name of the student from another class. If you wish, you may leave the room while the names are being written so that the spectator students know which names have been written, and then be brought in blindfolded for a dramatic denouement.

Magic trick #2: famous names

The illusion: Ask members of the class to call out the names of about ten famous people, past or present. You can adapt this trick to the curriculum by having students choose key words, dates and so on.

Each name/word is written on a separate card. The cards are then well mixed and you make a prediction on a pad of paper as to which card you think will be picked. A student selects one of the cards. He reads his selection aloud and the name you wrote on the pad is the same as the name read out.

How it's done: You will need ten small cards, a pad of paper and a hat. With everything at hand, ask someone to call out the name of a famous person/key word associated with the lesson topic. Write this down on one of the cards and drop it into the hat. Ask for another name/word. This time do not write the name/word that is called, but write the *first* name/word that was called. Now both cards in the hat have the same name written on them. As different names/words are called out you continue writing the original word on each card until you have about ten cards in the hat, all with the same word on them. Now write this word on the pad so that the class can't see it.

Place the pad where it can be seen, but with the writing facing away from the audience. Invite a student to come up and assist you. Shake the hat to mix the cards. Ask the student to reach into the hat and select one of the cards and read aloud the word written on it. After he or she does this, turn the pad around to show that the name selected was the same as the one you predicted. Be sure to destroy the slips after the trick so that no one can work out how you did it.

Magic trick #3: you WILL follow my instructions

The illusion: You reach into your pocket or desk drawer and start pulling out random objects – a pair of scissors, some keys, a whistle, a wristwatch, a flux capacitor, thumb screws, etc. You select three items (let's say the watch, the keys and the whistle) and place them on the desk.

You say: 'Jonny, you're going to pick one of these items and I'm going to make you pick the one I want you to pick using subliminal messaging. The *key* here, I'll say that again, the *key* here is to focus on one item and pick the one that *locks* [looks] right.' (You make it quite obvious that you are trying to suggest the keys to Jonny by highlighting the words *key* and *locks*.)

Jonny smiles a smile which says, 'I don't think so, sir,' and picks the watch. You look surprised but then say, 'Well, that's very interesting, Jonny. You obviously think you can ignore my instructions completely but you underestimate the power I have over you.' You point at a blank piece of paper on the desk and ask Jonny to turn it over. On the other side it reads 'You will pick the watch – told you!'

How it's done: You are actually covered no matter what object the student picks with this nifty little trick. If he picks the keys you direct him to look closely at the keys and read the key fob. On the key fob is written, 'Ha ha, I knew you'd pick the keys! Don't underestimate me.' By placing the keys with the fob facing down on the table he would not see this during the trick until he picks them up.

Similarly, if he picks the whistle, you ask him to look carefully at the ribbon to which the whistle is tied. Written clearly along it are the words, 'Ha ha, I knew you'd pick the whistle! Don't underestimate me.' Again, he would only see these words when his attention is drawn to them – after he has picked the item. If you happen to have a Dictaphone in your drawer a nice variation is to have a message pre-recorded: 'Ha ha, I knew you'd pick the Dictaphone …'

This trick is quite adaptable. You can use a whole range of topic related props and it also works with children not called Jonny.

You'll find a few more mind magic tricks you can use in class at: www.noisyclass.com/bookresources.

9. Include mini reviews

Mini reviews can be used to inject some energy into the lesson at any stage and are a very effective way to reinforce any piece of learning.

Joggers

Ask the whole class to stand up and get them jogging on the spot. Students have to continue jogging on the spot until sufficient (depending on the target number) relevant, topic related facts have been called out.

Fireworks

Tell students that a 'firework' is what you call it when a student jumps up from their seat and contributes something positive to the lesson – for example, by stating something they have learned so far in the lesson or during the last phase of work. Start a timer and tell students you want to see a number of fireworks from them in the next 30 or 60 seconds (any longer than that drags the activity out too long and enthusiasm starts to wane). Sometimes an incentive may be helpful: 'Okay, it's breaktime in ten minutes, but if you want your break I need to see 15 fireworks in the next 60 seconds.'

10. Include teach-backs

Teach-back activities are fun ways to encourage students to cement their learning by teaching others what they have been taught. Remember the saying, 'You never really learn anything until you teach it'? As well as helping students to learn new information, teach-back activities are great for the teacher too because they let you check for understanding and see how much your students have learned. They also give you a bit of free time (remember that?).

Ready, steady ... teach!

This is a great routine to build up with your students and can be used as a quick (and often extremely lively) review at the end of any phase of teacher-talk or explanation. It's very effective.

Explain to the students that whenever you call out the words 'Ready, steady ... teach!' (in your best Ainsley Harriott voice) they are to work with their allotted learning partner for 30 or 60 seconds to teach-back what they have learned moments before.

Learning partners should be numbered 1 and 2 because this teach-back has three phases:

Phase 1: After teaching the group the new information, the teacher asks if there are any questions before moving on in order to clarify the learning and eliminate misunderstandings during the next stage.

Phase 2: The teacher calls 'Ready, steady … *teach!*' and partner 1 immediately starts teaching partner 2 the new concept. It's important that they are encouraged to over-emphasise the key points with facial expressions and exaggerated hand gestures (humour makes learning stick) but also that they move through the information fairly briskly. For a difficult concept students are given up to a minute to teach-back the key points of the new information, but it is best to keep the activity brief – once they lose interest the effect is lost. This should be a fast paced, snappy review, nothing more.

Phase 3: The teacher brings the first session of teaching to a close (I like to use a 'honk-honk' bicycle horn to call attention and signify transitions) and have partners swap roles. On the second call of 'Ready, steady … *teach!*' partner 2 teaches partner 1. The partners then thank each other for being wonderful teachers and the lesson continues.

Chapter 12
Maintaining lesson flow

When students experience boredom, frustration or an interruption of any kind, varying levels of inappropriate behaviour can start to emerge. Their attention wanders, they start to work mechanically without giving much thought to what they are doing or they start fooling around. Once this happens, the teacher is going to be spending valuable time and energy regaining control and getting students back on task. In this chapter we're going to look at some ways to help keep students on task and minimise disruptions.

Use activity checklists

An activity checklist (or lesson outline) is simply a list of the activities that will be taking place during the lesson. What makes it work as a way of maintaining appropriate behaviour is when the list is on display and tasks are ticked off as they are completed. Boys, in particular, benefit from knowing exactly where they are up to in a lesson and what's coming next, and a checklist on display enables them to tell at a glance what they have achieved so far and what there is left to do.

Here is a very simple example of an activity checklist which you might stick up at the side of the board – it essentially consists of the main tasks associated with your lesson plan. It can be very calming for students who have problems maintaining attention to see the lesson progressing task by task.

- Starter – 5 minutes

- Video – 10 minutes

- Teacher demo – 5 minutes

- Pair work – 20 minutes

- Game – 10 minutes

- Plenary – 10 minutes

Once you have gone over this list, you can then direct the students to their next activity as and when they finish the preceding task. When they know what is coming next, the transition is much smoother.

Stockpile emergency activities and early finisher tasks

All lessons go wrong from time to time, but with a tough group it is highly likely that an activity you have spent all night planning will completely bomb. When this happens you need to have other suitable 'emergency' activities ready to hand to occupy idle, bored or frustrated minds. Fun, meaningful and engaging activities can be compiled for any topic using the Internet and/or teacher resource books. You can issue a pack of these activities to each student for them to work on whenever they have spare time, or keep them to hand for when a planned lesson task doesn't work out. Create two or three differentiated versions of each activity to make sure that students at all levels are able to access these resources and practise their skills.

Use frequent structured breaks

Brain breaks, stretches, energisers, water breaks and serotonin moments (e.g. jokes, quick games, novel/quirky stories, funny videos) all have an important place in a lesson with a noisy class. Tough kids often have short attention spans, and even if you are fortunate enough to have found an activity on which they are totally focused they will need occasional structured breaks of some sort every 20 minutes or so. These can be used at the beginning of a group session as well as in the middle or at the end. They are also a wonderful way to build group cohesion and stimulate interaction because they depend on the group's cooperation and participation.

Please don't make the mistake of discounting energisers as a waste of time. You will waste far more time having to deal with students who are bored, listless, lacking in energy and in need of an activity change. Energisers, when used appropriately, can maintain the attention of an otherwise troublesome class by providing the means to quickly refocus and re-engage jaded or irritated young minds.

Here are a few brain breaks and energisers you can try.

 ## Brain break: I'm the captain of the ship

Time: 5–15 minutes

Purpose: To develop listening skills and settle a group who have lost interest in an activity or become too boisterous.

Directions:

1. Ask everyone to sit quietly and say: 'I'm the captain of the ship and I'm packing some carrots. What would you like to pack?' Only items that begin with the first letter of the speaker's name (e.g. captain/carrots) can be packed but this fact is not explained to the students – they have to work it out for themselves.

2. Invite students, one at a time, to suggest another object to pack for the journey. For example, the first student might say, 'My name is John and I'm packing some shorts,' to which you would reply, 'Oh, I'm so sorry, John. I'm afraid you can't take your shorts but you could take a jumper if you wanted to.' Extra emphasis can be given to the first letter as the game progresses, if necessary.

3. Continue inviting students to offer an object to add to the packed items list.

When a student guesses the pattern, instruct them not to tell other students what it is. Instead, ask them to keep playing the game and adding more items to the list. At first it may be difficult to get the group to settle into this activity, but gradually the intrigue will build up and they will all want to take part and find the secret to taking their items on board the ship. If you have problems getting them quiet at the start of the activity, write the opening statement on the board rather than saying it out loud.

As a variation, rather than picking words which start with the same letter, you could choose words which have a double consonant (e.g. hammer, bottle, pebble). Alternatively, you could include an accompanying code or gesture – for example, innocently say, 'Okay …' prior to the actual sentence every time it's your turn to speak ('Okay … I'm the captain of the ship and I'm packing …'). Only students who realise that they have to add 'Okay' will be able to take their items. Or you could subtly scratch your nose or ear as you say your sentence. Students will have to pay extra attention to spot these little nuances.

Energiser: Mini/maxi stretches

Time: 4–5 minutes

Purpose: To refocus a group, to provide some light relief following an intense working period, to raise energy levels, to raise spirits and to have some fun. This energiser has the additional benefit of being easy to relate to the lesson content.

Directions:

1. Ask the whole class to stand up.

2. Demonstrate a mini stretch by moving a small part of your body (e.g. curl a lip, twitch a finger) compared with a maxi stretch (e.g. reach for the ceiling, lift a leg). While demonstrating the stretch, simultaneously state out loud one fact that is topic related.

3. Everyone then copies the stretch while repeating the same fact. The teacher then nominates another student to model a mini or maxi stretch while stating another topic related fact. This student must then call on another to do the same.

4. Perform four or five stretches before continuing with the lesson (or pulling a muscle – whichever comes first).

Energiser: Box breathing

Time: 2–3 minutes

Purpose: To refocus a group, to provide some light relief following an intense working period or to settle and calm a lively group.

Directions: Start by inviting everyone to take ten special, calming breaths. Some groups get silly at this point so you might give them a little background on why they are being asked to do this. Tell them this is an ancient yoga technique now used by highly advanced athletes and NASA astronauts to gain mental clarity and relaxation – and may possibly even develop their sixth sense and psychic capabilities. That is often sufficient to arouse their curiosity and get them to try the activity.

1. Ask the students to take a slow breath in for the count of four. (Watch out for students breathing in too deeply. There should be no effort involved in this process – the idea is to relax while doing so.)

2. They then hold their breath for the count of four.

3. They then breathe out for the count of four.

4. At the end of the exhalation they hold their breath once again for the count of four before repeating the cycle.

After two or three cycles, students will find their own rate and rhythm and should start to settle. Encourage them to close their eyes as this helps them focus more on their breathing.

This breathing cycle in the ratio of 4:4:4:4 is actually very calming. You can use it yourself before any lesson with a really tough group. (Or, if the group is really tough, before handing in your resignation.)

Energiser: Dance off

Time: 10–30 seconds

Materials: A CD or MP3 full of top disco tunes – the type guaranteed to get you on your feet and shaking your booty … um … daddio.

Purpose: A brilliant, if not essential, way to add hilarity to all your lessons while injecting learning boosting oxygen into your students' bodies.

Directions:

1. Students should work in table groups.

2. Explain that you will be playing a tune at various points throughout the lesson. It should be sufficiently cheesy – anything from *Saturday Night Fever* will do. Let them hear a sample of the tune so they know what's coming. Tell them that as soon as they hear the tune they must get on their feet and strut their stuff, throwing out the best moves they can muster.

3. Allocate points quickly at the end of each 'dance off' – only giving points to table groups in which all members of the team are on their feet.

4. Keep a record of points and award a prize at the end of the week to the winning team (e.g. early finish, less homework).

 You can download some ready-made energisers and brain break activities from: www.noisyclass.com/bookresources.

Set individual work targets

This is without doubt one of the very best strategies I have ever come across for keeping challenging students on task. Work targets seem to have an almost magical calming effect on students and can improve their initial attitude towards a task and/or re-engage them when their attention starts to wander.

Targets work on the principle that some students can only cope with small chunks of achievable/appropriate work at a time. When they are presented with a large or confusing task, the fear of failure kicks in and manifests as a range of work avoidance strategies – from point blank refusal to pick up a pen all the way through to flinging their chair across the room, kicking the waste bin and stropping out of the room, as well as pretty much any other act of silliness or general disruption you can think of. Targets give students confidence in their abilities to complete a task; they make success achievable and attainable – a rare opportunity and a huge relief for many challenged young people.

To give you an example, let's say our old friend Jonny is messing around and being mildly disruptive. Rather than nag him to get on with his work, or threaten him if he doesn't, we give him a realistic work target: 'Jonny it's two o'clock. By ten past you need to have completed your work to this mark (put pencil mark in his book) – that's your target.' Or, 'Jonny, this is your target – I want you to get to number 6 in the next ten minutes.'

I know it sounds too simple to even bother with, but I've had whole groups of normally inattentive students literally pleading with me to give them a work target. This single strategy made a huge difference to my relationships with my toughest classes.

 It's best to issue targets quietly because some students are self-conscious about being given smaller targets than their peers, while others will argue if they feel they have been given too much work. In every class there are badly behaved students who are, in fact, very capable. With these children I explain, in private, that I'll be giving them a bigger target (more work) than anyone else – for example, 'Jonny, I'm going to set you a high target today because I know you can excel at this. I wouldn't be doing my job well if I didn't give you the chance to show me what you can do. Okay?' If I did this without explanation there would be an uproar, but by taking the student to one side before the lesson they become much more cooperative.

Avoid excessive teacher-talk

Giving too many verbal instructions throughout a lesson can become very distracting for students. I see new teachers doing this a lot – they rush through the instructions for an activity and then keep interrupting and stopping the group from working while they shout more instructions which they either forgot or didn't explain properly. Eventually students tune out which makes it difficult to get their attention when you have something more important to say.

If you are explaining a complex task you need to break it down into very simple steps (or single teaching points) and go through each of these carefully – ensuring students have completely understood at each stage.

Try writing down your instructions as a concise, one-step-at-a-time checklist, cue card or reminder sheet and give one to each student at the start of a task. Then, rather than constantly telling them what to do, you can just refer them to the checklist.

Provide adequate support

Support is an aspect of classroom management which can benefit from having a routine – after all, students needing your attention is something that happens a hundred times a day. The pressure on the teacher can be immense when half a class of young people are all demanding immediate and individual attention at the same time, but students aren't going to learn to solve their own problems if they get used to enjoying support and assistance every time they ask for (or demand) it.

A self-check/partner check/teacher check routine frees up the teacher from attending to what are often unnecessary, time consuming questions – and it teaches the students to rely on themselves and each other. Students are told that whenever they have a question they must first self-check their work again to see if they can find a way of solving the problem. If they can't they must then ask their learning partner or other group members. Finally, if they still can't find a solution, they can ask the teacher.

You can have routines like these in place to deal with all kinds of frequently occurring problems and questions, such as 'what to do if you haven't brought the right equipment', 'what to do if you finish early', 'what to do if someone is annoying you', 'how to label diagrams correctly', 'what to do if you come in late', 'how to use equipment' and so on. And the more you have in place, the less time you'll have to spend giving the same instructions again and again.

I've found one of the best times to offer support to a chatty student is actually prior to the lesson (one to one in the corridor), and the 'pre-agreed private signal' is a great way to show that you care about their success:

> Jonny, can I have a quick word? Listen, I've been noticing you get very chatty in these lessons and I'm wondering if there's anything I can do to help? I'm wondering if you're even aware that you're doing it sometimes. Anyway, I don't want to be on your case all the time telling you to be quiet, and I really want you to get through the term without any more detentions, so how about I help you to get on top of this problem? Every time I see you talking out of turn, rather than shout at you, I'll just give you this hand signal/ slip of paper. Nobody needs to know – it's just a private signal between you and me. Shall we try this for a couple of lessons and see how you go?

Ask spot questions

There are obviously times when we need to explain things to the class, but we can make teacher-talk time interactive and use it to maintain lesson flow by constantly directing questions at different individuals. It keeps them on their toes and paying attention because they quickly catch on that they could be asked a question at any time.

Two ways to improve spot questioning techniques

1. Always say the pupil's name **after** the question

If you say, 'Daniel, how do we know the water is boiling?' the other pupils will relax and switch off before you've even finished asking the question because they know you're directing it at Daniel. The correct way to ask the question would be, 'How do we know the water is boiling?' Pause, look around the room, and then name the pupil you wish to answer.

2. If a student can't answer a question, don't just ask someone else

If a student can't initially answer a question, keep asking it in simpler and simpler terms until they can give you an answer. This is essential if you are to stop pupils from getting into the habit of opting out. They have given the (perhaps legitimate) excuse that they don't understand, so it's up to you to help them understand by rephrasing the question until they do.

Teacher: Describe the process through which plants produce their own food please ... David.

David: (Blank stare)

Teacher: Okay, tell me what a plant must have in order to produce food.

David: (Blank stare)

Teacher: Right, a plant produces its own food but it needs to take in certain raw materials. First of all, tell me the name of the substance it takes in through its roots.

David: Water.

Teacher: Well done, now tell me the name of the gas that plants take in through their leaves.

... and so on.

Your pupils need to realise that they must take part in the lesson and that taking part is a pain-free exercise. If you allow them to get away with not giving an answer, other pupils will follow this trend.

Use a 'noise level meter'

Background music makes a great noise level meter. Have it playing fairly softly in the background and assign one student per table group with the job of making sure the music is always audible. Once they can no longer hear it, they know they are too loud and they must tell their teammates to quieten down; if they can hear the music then the volume is okay.

Another option is to have a visible reminder on the board or wall. This could be as simple as putting a sign up on the wall ('You're too noisy') whenever talking turns into shouting, or you could be a little more creative with a colour scheme similar to traffic lights. A green card means levels are appropriate, orange means they're getting a little bit too loud and red is way too loud.

Instead of nagging kids to be quiet, just walk over to the wall and change the card to reflect the current noise level. In time, the students will start to look out for you doing this and they will remind each other to keep quiet when the orange card goes up. If the room is too noisy, put up the red card and tell students they must now work independently in silence for five minutes. If they manage that then you can then put the green card back up. A visual reminder like this develops responsibility and encourages children to monitor their own noise levels.

Know how to get their attention when lesson flow has been disrupted

If you've seen the film *Dangerous Minds*, in which Michelle Pfeiffer plays the committed and gifted teacher LouAnne Johnson, you may remember the opening scene in which LouAnne meets her class for the first time.[1] After being sworn at and verbally abused she walks out into the corridor, almost in tears, and is consoled by a seasoned colleague from the next classroom. 'I can't teach these kids!' she splutters, in desperation. 'Sure you can, LouAnne,' he answers, 'all you've got to do is get their attention.'

If you lose the attention of your group, or struggle to get their attention at the start of lessons, here's a nifty collection of ideas which may help.

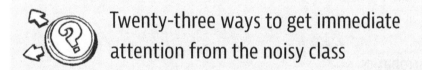 Twenty-three ways to get immediate attention from the noisy class

1. The unexpected

Done correctly this idea never fails. All you have to do is present the students with something they are not expecting and then hold back on the explanation. Kids are naturally very inquisitive creatures and will be desperate to know why you've arranged the classroom differently, switched on coloured lights, set up some weird equipment, arranged some party food on the main table or walked in backwards with your underwear on your head. This puts the power

---

1 A fabrication by Hollywood producers; I have spoken with the real-life LouAnne and know for a fact that she never once ran out of a classroom in tears. After nine years of military service, she was not one to be intimidated by a group of difficult teenagers: she faced them down, made them sit and explained the rules of engagement to them. They had driven three teachers out of the classroom before her, but she stayed in that particular room for five years. That said, this movie moment illustrates a point, so let's recount the fiction for a moment.

ball very much back in your court: 'I'll explain everything … as soon as you've all stopped talking.'

2. Pictionary

An abstract picture sketched on the board with the words, 'Can you guess what this is?' will catch students' attention as they walk into the room. Don't say anything but as soon as someone guesses what it is, give them a card with a key word related to the subject topic and get them to come up and draw a sketch to represent the word on the card. The person who guesses what it is swaps places with them and is given a new key word. You can formalise this game by creating teams and setting time limits or you may prefer it as a quick impromptu starter.

3. Acrobatics

If you can do a cartwheel, flip nimbly across the front of the room and round off with a double somersault while juggling kittens, then (a) you're probably in the wrong profession and (b) you'll definitely get their attention. I tried this once (without the kittens).

4. Musical instrument/noise maker

Playing a musical instrument such as a tambourine, cowbell, guitar, piano or kazoo gives a non-aggressive but very audible signal that you want every-one's attention. And you'll certainly get it if you walk into the room carrying a piano. Here are a few other noise makers to consider:

- Clapping: If you haven't got an instrument you can use your hands, but be careful if some students are prone to silliness. Rather than randomly clapping every time you want them to listen, try clapping out a rhythm that they then have to clap back to you.

- Smoke alarm: Keep one of these in your drawer and 'test' it whenever you want total silence. If you plan on doing this regularly it might be an idea to issue ear plugs.

- Bugle horn: Taking the noise maker idea to its ultimate conclusion, I use an old bicycle horn during seminars/workshops and also in schools when I'm working with students. It adds a bit of humour (think circus clown) and cuts through chatter and classroom noise like a knife through a custard pie.

You might also consider linking the sound to a particular activity so that you have different signals/sounds for different actions, such as sitting on the carpet (for younger students), putting pens down, clearing away, lining up and giving you their dinner money.

5. The quiet game

Somehow, when you just add the word 'game' to a request, students will generally sit up and listen. You can get the immediate attention of a noisy group by shouting (or writing on the board if they are already much louder than you), 'Let's play the SHOUTING GAME and see how much noise you can *really* make. As soon as you're quiet I'll explain the rules.'

Once you have their attention, explain that they can have five seconds to make as much noise as they want – but after the five seconds, when you raise your hand, they are to be completely silent and you'll time them to see how fast they respond. Repeat the game a couple of times and you should find that the habit of immediately becoming silent whenever you raise your hand is sufficiently embedded. This is surprisingly effective but you may want to warn staff in rooms nearby.

6. The music box

Buy an inexpensive music box and wind it up at the start of the lesson in front of the students. Tell them that whenever they are noisy or off task, or whenever you need their attention, you will open the box and let the music play until they are silent. If, at the end of the day, there is any music left, they earn a reward.

7. Hands up!

Say to students: 'Next time I want you to be quiet I will put my hand in the air. The last person to put their hand in the air and stop talking will have their name put on the board/will have to come and sit at the front for ten minutes (or some other appropriate consequence).' You might also add: 'If you put your hand up but carry on talking, I find that even more disrespectful so you will have to come and see me at break.'

8. I've got my 'eye' on you

Bags of toy plastic eyes can be bought very cheaply in craft and hobby shops. They move, they look silly and your students will love them! Spell out your messages in eye code:

One eye on a table = I'm keeping an eye on you.

Two eyes = I've got both my eyes on you – be careful.

Three eyes = a consequence.

Students are prone to play with these when you place them on a table with a group, so a laminated chart on the wall with each group's name and a space to add the eyes works just as well.

9. Shhh, you'll wake the baby ...

This is one for very young students. Position a baby doll in the corner of the room. Designate a 'noise level monitor' to pick it up and go to front of class and say, 'Shhh, you'll wake the baby!' whenever noise levels get too high.

10. Stop clock

Whenever younger students start talking set the clock going. At the same time keep a record on the board of who is talking and apply a strike after their name:

John   /
Kate   /
Jacob   /

The next time there's chatter you add an additional strike to those students who are talking. Then, at the end of the lesson, you take the time they have wasted from the stop clock during the lesson and keep back whoever has three strikes for that time over break. Anyone who has four strikes gets a consequence.

11. The singing horses

This is a fun strategy but it won't work with all groups and it has a shelf life. If you type 'singing horses' into Google you will find the game which can be displayed on the interactive whiteboard – when you click on the horses they sing. You can start with all four singing at the start of a lesson (or during an activity) while students get themselves ready. Stop the horses one by one so that by the time the last horse stops all the students have to be silent. Anyone talking when the horses have stopped faces a consequence, such as moving to a desk at the front of the room for five minutes.

12. Rhymes with actions

Example 1: You call, 'Hands on heads, hands on hips, hands on shoulders, fingers on lips', to get their attention and then repeat it a second time along with the students while performing the actions.

Example 2: You call, 'One, two, three – eyes on me!' The students respond with a loud, 'One, two – eyes on you!'

Example 3: You call, 'If you hear me, clap your hands' (those that don't hear will stop to see why other students are clapping). If the noise continues, add other actions – for example, 'If you hear me snap your fingers, wiggle your nose, wink, and so on'.

13. Sir, yes sir!

If you've seen the drill scenes in *Full Metal Jacket* or *An Officer and a Gentleman*, you'll know exactly how this one works. You might also want to warn teachers in any adjoining classrooms!

Teacher:	Whenever I need you to listen really closely to me I'm going to say one word, *atten-tion!* And I want you all to respond by shouting, 'Sir, yes sir!' (John Wayne drawl) Okay?
Students:	Okay sir!
Teacher:	Atteeeeeen-tion!
Students:	Sir, yes sir! (or Miss, yes miss!)

14. All stand

At the first sign of talking or murmuring, pause and say, 'Stand up please'. Get them to stand behind their chairs while you continue with the lesson.

15. Reward quiet students

Praise quiet students throughout the lesson. Make a list of these individuals and let them go slightly earlier than the other students. Don't make a fuss, just let them go early while those who were talking are kept back for a minute or two. A sanction doesn't have to be particularly harsh in order for it to be effective. In this case, two minutes stood behind a desk while their peers trot out to the bus will be excruciating for some students. You will only have to do it a few times for the message to get through – good behaviour is rewarded.

16. Start the clock

Write on the board: 'This lesson is 60 minutes long and you won't leave this room until you've had the pleasure of 60 minutes of my awesome teaching. I'll stop the clock whenever you hold up the lesson and add that time to the end of the lesson.' Start the clock when they are quiet but stop it whenever they interrupt.

17. Whisper

When the classroom noise level is getting out of control, whisper something along the lines of, 'If you can hear my voice raise your hand, and you'll get five minutes of free time at the end of the day'. That way, anyone who is listening will hear and get the reward but those who were not will be left seething with jealousy.

18. B-R-I-L-L-I-A-N-T

Remember, it is better to focus on the behaviour you want to see rather than that you don't. Tell the students at the beginning of class that every time they are listening attentively, staying on task and so on, they will get one letter of the word BRILLIANT written on the board. If they get all of the letters by the end of the lesson they get a class reward.

19. Secret agent

This is a great tool for encouraging participation in lessons and for building class camaraderie. Here's how it works:

- Each student is given a secret agent card on entry to the classroom. This will immediately stimulate curiosity and gives you an effective way to get students settled and listening once they are in the room. Say, 'I'll tell you what this card is for as soon as you are all quiet.'

- Ask the students to write their name on the card and that one student will be selected at random to be the secret agent. You can then put the cards in a hat for dramatic effect or to save time just pick a name from the class list/register.

- None of the students must know the identity of the secret agent – not even the secret agent. Tell the class that as long as this student has a good lesson (you can formalise this by giving them a behaviour or work target of some sort), the entire class will receive a reward.

The beauty of this idea is that because none of the students know the identity of the secret agent, it usually results in *all* students trying hard to achieve the stated target. Also, if the student in question does not have a good lesson or reach the target for some reason, they aren't held responsible by the rest of the group. So, this little gem not only encourages good behaviour and participation but also promotes teamwork and group cohesion.

 You can download a set of ready-made secret agent cards for photocopying from: www.noisyclass.com/bookresources.

20. DJ

Play some nice relaxing music in the background – it's amazing how many students actually start requesting classical tunes once they've heard them a few times. Turn the music off when you want their attention or to signify the end of a period of work/transition into a new task.

21. Anchors

This is a clever technique – it works like magic. It takes a little time to set up an anchor but once established they can literally work wonders with challenging groups. Anchors can be used to automate a variety of teaching processes and can be locations around the room, pieces of music, body positions, props such as silly hats, actions and so on.

Here's an example of how a location anchor can be used to get attention from noisy students whenever you want to tell them something:

- Pick a spot where you are going to stand and can be seen by the whole class. Tell students that whenever you stand on this spot they must immediately stop talking and sit in silence.

- Try to make a game of this – have a few practice tries where you let them talk while you walk around the room and then walk towards the mark. Look at them to let them know you will soon be on the mark and then jump with a smile. Do this a few times and your anchor should be sufficiently embedded. From this point on you should only need to walk towards the mark on the floor and the students will suspend talking to hear what you have to say.

- Towards the end of the session jump on the anchor spot one last time before making the following announcement: 'Because you've all worked so well I'm going to let you all go two minutes early.'

22. Fun verbal routine

The beauty of this routine is that the students get to make a lot of noise. It's a very effective way of getting everyone's attention very quickly without being confrontational. Explain to students that whenever you sing out certain words they must respond as a group. So, the teacher calls out: 'Daaa da da da …', and the students respond: 'Daaaaaaaaaaaaaaaaa!'

23. Teams

Put your students into table group teams. Get them to come up with a team name and perhaps a logo, graffiti tag or coat of arms to get them working together. Put a score sheet on the wall and keep a tally whenever you ask for silence or need their attention. Whichever team is still talking when the others are silent loses a point. Team spirit, peer pressure and the element of competition tends to make this work well with some more malleable groups.

Chapter 13
Dealing with problems

Despite our best intentions, and no matter how thorough we have been in terms of implementing our preventive strategies, there are always going to be problems in any lesson – particularly with the noisy class. In this chapter we'll look at some ways you can deal with those you are likely to face most often. You'll notice that some of the ideas have been mentioned elsewhere in this book; my hope is that by repeating them here you can see how they can be used to address specific issues.

Dealing with students who won't complete work in class

When students won't get started or when their efforts tail off during a lesson, it's probably down to one or more of the following:

- Being distracted by other students or outside interruptions.

- Losing interest in work that is too easy or has become repetitive.

- Getting frustrated with work that is too difficult. (If they aren't gaining a sense of achievement they will soon switch off – remember how important empowerment is?)

- Something going wrong with the equipment they are using which breaks their concentration and takes them out of 'work mode'.

- Discomfort – is the room too warm and stuffy? Is it too cold? Is there a bad smell floating around? (If you're teaching teenage boys it's highly likely.)

- Waning energy/becoming lethargic.

- Finding that other students are getting all the attention. (They may feel the need to switch off/act up to get some negative teacher attention if they see other students taking up the teacher's time.)

As you can see there are several possible reasons. This list is by no means exhaustive but each of those possible reasons has one thing in common – they can all be alleviated or prevented with good planning.

So how do you plan ahead for students who lose their motivation to work during lessons?

 ## Take efforts to minimise and prepare for distractions

Distractions can take many forms – some avoidable, some not – but there are ways we can reduce the chances of occurrences and minimise their effects. Here are a few common distractions and ways to deal with them.

Breaking wind

Boys will be boys, and some of them seem to take great delight in breaking wind during lessons, usually – for extra comic effect – when everyone in the room is silent. We can't control what he eats beforehand but we can reduce the chances of this happening by giving the student sufficient attention so he doesn't feel as much need to cause a disruption. We should also have a good plan in place to deal with this particular distraction when it does occur. Iron-clad consequences are the best way.

> Teacher: Jonny, we don't do that in lessons. Please pack up your things and move to the seat at the back. If it happens again you'll go to time out (or come back at break for five minutes – whatever sanction you have in place).
>
> Jonny: I couldn't help it.

Teacher: That may be true, Jonny, but it's something we all have to learn to control. Move now please or, as I said, you'll be going to time out.

The trick, as with any confrontation like this, is to show as little emotion as possible, not get drawn into a discussion or argument and to follow up *every* time.

If you don't know who the culprit was you can use a slightly different plan. Open a window, show as little concern as possible and tell students who are overreacting to be quiet and stop being silly. Have an activity on hand with which to refocus them.

Note: No matter how earnest the protest that they 'couldn't help it', I would always assume it was deliberate and issue the consequence. Once you allow leeway for an 'accident' the rest have a perfect excuse for a repeat performance.

Asking to go to the toilet

This is the favoured 'work avoidance' strategy in many classrooms and you're going to need a plan for dealing with it. My personal view is that anyone can hold on for an hour (the duration of most lessons), and if they can't, they need to learn how to. I know there has to be provision made for some individuals on health grounds but unless they have a note from parents and/or the school has been made aware of this problem, all students should receive the same consideration. They are given an opportunity to go to the toilet before the lesson starts and then nobody goes during the lesson. If that's too draconian for you, you can try being lenient on a student who claims they are about to 'wet themselves' and then come up with another plan to deal with the five students who say they have the same problem ten minutes later. It is better to have one rule, and stick to it.

If you're worried about denying students their rights and receiving formal complaints from parents there are other alternatives such as issuing 'toilet passes' or setting a limit of one toilet visit per lesson per student and recording visits in a file or the back of the student's book. In each case the student should be given a definite time by which they should be back in the room (written in their book/on the card) and they should take this with them. This will enable other staff, such as tutors and other teachers, to monitor trends – as well as preventing the student from being wrongly accused of wandering if caught in the corridor.

Other students

It is actually fairly easy to prevent and deal with problems caused by other students. Separate individuals who are likely to distract each other, move the liveliest students to the front of the room so you can keep a close eye on them and have back-up/alternative lesson tasks on hand to refocus those who lose concentration.

Plan for students getting bored or frustrated

Plan for frequent changes of task (every 15–20 minutes – less with low ability groups) and/or increasingly higher levels of challenge for able students, with simpler alternatives for the less able. Prepare tasks which meet different learning styles and know your students so that you can offer them targeted work which is likely to introduce quick teach-back and discussion activities to break monotony. Remember, once they switch off it's going to be tough getting them switched on again – you *must* plan ahead and pre-empt boredom. As soon as you detect the warning signs, act quickly to keep them on task. That is the time to change the activity, begin a quick energiser or just offer them some quiet encouragement or support.

Give limited choices rather than confrontational commands

The reason why limited choices work so well is that they give students an element of control over the situation rather than making them feel they are being forced into a decision. Students, some more than others, have a need for autonomy; they hate being forced to do anything, and if they don't feel they are in control to some extent they will argue.

For example, if you tell such a student to complete ten questions from the textbook, *right now* (and stand over them scowling), they will almost certainly find something to argue about – either that ten questions are too many, that the subject is boring or that you should go and pick on someone else.

These students find it incredibly difficult to back down, especially in front of their friends, so the more we boss them around, the more we become embroiled in a power struggle with them. Giving them a limited choice takes the sting out of the situation and gives them a way of complying without losing face (i.e. it is them making a decision, rather than us telling them what to do). In this way responsibility is passed to the student.

Here are some examples:

> Jonny, do you want to carry on sitting with your friend and get on with your work quietly, or do you want to come and sit at the front with me and work quietly? The choice is yours. I'll go and help Paul for a minute and then come back to see what you've decided.

> Jonny, you can play this game by the rules or you can sit out and get on with some written work at the desk at the back. It's up to you – your choice.

> Jonny, you can sit on the chair properly, without swinging and with all four chair legs on the floor, or you can sit on the floor and do your work there for ten minutes while you remember how chairs are supposed to be used. Your choice.

Dealing with inappropriate comments

There are always going to be students who try to make us feel uncomfortable by asking inappropriate, personal and silly questions. This is especially common when we get a new class to teach – whether it's the start of term or a cover lesson – and it is a scenario which must be dealt with swiftly or else your control over the class can be severely eroded.

Why are you late, sir?

Were you out last night, sir?

Where did you go, sir?

Do you drink, sir?

Were you drinking last night, sir?

Is that why you're late, sir?

Did you pull, sir?

Does your wife know, sir?

Have you got a wife, sir?

Is she nice looking, sir?

... and so on.

They do this to gain attention, hold up lessons and look good in front of their friends. They do it to try to find our weaknesses, to embarrass us and ultimately to wind us up. Sometimes they try to shock us in front of their peers as a way of displaying or increasing their status and sometimes they just want to have a laugh. Other times it may be because they feel they have known us long enough to warrant being over-familiar.

Such situations, harmless as they may seem at first, need to be stopped early before they get out of hand. If you go along with the first few questions more and more students will get drawn in, and once that happens the comments get worse – becoming sillier, ruder and more personal until the situation becomes very difficult to control. The result is, at best, a very annoyed and embarrassed member of staff, a loss of respect, damaged relationships and a class of very excited students

– some of whom are likely to be given sanctions they will consider unfair and which could have been avoided.

One way to deal with this type of questioning is to take the attention away from the student as soon as possible. The following techniques are excellent for doing this and should be used whenever you are faced with inappropriate questions or insults from a student.

 ## Take the attention away

Calmly state that the conversation is inappropriate and must stop

Say: 'OK, stop there. The comments are inappropriate/unacceptable. You need to think before saying things like that to a member of staff.' Make the statement without emotion and then move on with the lesson. It should be a complete brush off. Don't get drawn into a conversation with this student and don't respond to any more of their comments – you've dealt with them and they deserve no more of your attention.

Create a diversion such as a quick demonstration, introducing a new topic/game etc.

Say: 'Look this way everyone, please, I set this up earlier' or 'Okay, for this game you need a blue pen and a piece of scrap paper ...' Once again, the secret is to move on from the questions straight away and change the focus of attention. In order to be able to do this swiftly and not get caught out trying to think of suitable alternative activities, you really should have a resource file (either in your head or hard copy) of interesting and engaging games and fill-in activities.

Make a public note of the student's comments

Take out a pen and paper and say: 'I'm writing your comments down. I'm recording what you say so that I don't make a mistake when I explain your behaviour to other people.'

Dealing with abusive language

Children need to be very clear about the consequences of their use of bad language. If there is no school policy in place then use your own – and stick to it. That way they will eventually learn that they can't get away with it.

The oft-quoted strategy of staying calm applies equally well here. No matter how profane the offence (and you don't need me to tell you how creative they can be), try not to lose your temper. Let your chosen consequence do the job for you. Calmly state, 'That's a minute you owe me' (or whatever your sanction is for this scenario), mark it down and carry on with the lesson. Don't raise your voice while doing so as this can be read as the emotional response they are probably trying to trigger.

If swearing is a regular occurrence then the consequence needs to begin quite small. That may sound like double-dutch but if the air turns blue every two minutes in your classroom you can't dish out final tier punishments for every offence. If you begin with, 'Okay, that's a detention!' you are limiting your options for a follow-up (as well as risking having an entire class in detention!).

I once took a post in a residential unit for children with emotional and behavioural difficulties (EBD) and was stunned at the liberal attitude some staff had towards swearing in Year 10 and Year 11 groups. I had worked in very strict EBD settings prior to that and I decided that despite most of the staff's liberal attitude to foul language, I wasn't having it. It took me a few weeks but eventually there was no swearing in my class.

I did it by being totally consistent (making sure *every* incidence of swearing was addressed) and by making time to build up strong relationships with the boys in the group. I spent time with them after lessons – playing football and other games with them at breaktime, helping them with their work at lunchtime and after school, going out on evening trips and so on. I know what you're thinking and, yes, it did involve a lot of extra work, but the results justified it. It meant I only had to say, 'Oi, pack the language in', and they would immediately apologise and comply – they respected me because they knew I cared about them and because I had taken the time to get to know them. Eventually it ceased to be a problem at all – and these kids were the roughest of the rough!

 ## Strategies to manage swearing

Host a discussion session

Give students an opportunity to discuss the issue of swearing and set their own ground rules. Let them debate what they would or would not find acceptable, and what they would do about 'offenders'. Discuss with the class how we convey respect: how does the way we speak express respect or disrespect, care or disdain? What message is it sending when we use foul language? How should we speak, and why? What impression would others have of us if we used foul language in public – for example, in a restaurant with our girlfriend/boyfriend? Is that how we want to be viewed? What would be the advantages/disadvantages of being viewed negatively by others?

Refuse to be drawn in

Students will say, 'Oh, but we use this kind of language all the time' or 'My mum and dad say …' Respond by saying, 'Maybe so, but we do not speak like that in this class. I don't use that kind of language with you. I don't expect you to use that kind of language here in this classroom. Okay? Thank you.'

Don't make a big deal about it

Remember, this student is probably trying to provoke a reaction. Rather than show your disgust, first ensure the other students are occupied then take the offender aside and calmly deal with them out of earshot of the rest of the class.

Set up a 'swear box'

You can't take their money but you can hit them where it hurts by depriving them of merits, time and computer use. For each offence put a token in your own version of the box (or chart), with sanctions taking effect when the pre-arranged threshold is reached.

Engage support from parents

Try to encourage parents/guardians to follow up at home by encouraging polite language and discouraging swearing. You could suggest that *Breaking Bad* probably isn't the kind of family drama they should be watching, but probably better to just explain that incidents of inappropriate language are a problem in lessons and will become more of a problem for the student in future if they aren't checked.

Dealing with the disruptive joker

The joker is desperate for attention. His smart remarks, rude comments, smutty gestures, witty retorts and wisecracks may be funny (unfortunately, some class comedians really are amusing) but they are often a smokescreen to mask frustration, disappointment, low self-esteem and an inability to fit in.

Here are some suggestions to deal with the class joker.

Make sure he knows the extent of the problem

Often this student won't be aware of the problem he is causing – he thinks everything is okay because he's getting a few laughs. Explaining to him in private that he is actually starting to annoy the majority of his peers can have a dramatic effect – because this is the opposite of his desired effect. Impress on him that he may well be turning other students against him by acting in this way and that you don't want to see this happen. Tell him you have a nifty set of consequences which you will implement with the sole intention of helping him kick his silly and disruptive habit.

Explain consequences clearly

Make sure he knows exactly what will happen if he continues disrupting the lesson. Be sure to tell him this is not a personal vendetta against him, but it's the only way you know to help him remember how to behave in lessons and succeed.

Try not to show emotion when reprimanding him

Because of the dire craving for attention the last thing you want to do is reward the joker with an outburst, regardless of how many of your buttons he has pressed. Instead, issue consequences calmly and without any fuss every time he acts inappropriately. Don't give in to his protests either – just take the wind out of his sails with the following lines: 'I've told you what is happening. You made your choice. If you want to talk more about this we can do it later – come and see me after school, I'll be in my room. Now get on with your work.' And then turn your back, click your heels and march off into the sunset. Or back to your desk, whichever is nearer.

Remember the positive alternative

We've already established that this student wants attention so you should be ready and eager to pay some out – but only when he does something right. Praise is a very effective management strategy and you should award him with as much attention as you can possibly muster when he is settled and working – throw confetti, bring in a brass band, jump on the table and shout with joy, but only when he has deserved it. If you can stick to the 'no attention and no fuss consequence' for inappropriate behaviour and 'immediate sincere attention' for the right behaviour, you can see miracles occur surprisingly quickly.

Creative ways to deal with inappropriate mobile phone use

Policies regarding mobile phones vary from setting to setting so the way you address this problem will depend on the school/college's overall viewpoint. If the establishment you're working in has a definite rule and consequences in place regarding the use of phones you can treat this as any usual behaviour problem and consistently stick to the policy.

Mobiles can be such a huge problem, with students being so passionate about their phones that enforcing the rules can be difficult. Here are four strategies you could consider.

1. Pre-empt and negate the need to take emergency calls

Students will always give the excuse that they need to be able to receive emergency calls from home on their phones. Maybe they do, maybe they don't, but by sending a card home with the school/college number on it and the assurance that any message will be passed on to the student immediately you remove any need for them to have a phone.

2. Offer texting time

Texting time can only be used when the school has a clear procedure regarding the use of phones. If fixed rules are in place prohibiting their use you obviously can't be seen to openly abuse them. However, if the issue is left up to you to sort out in your own way, and if texting in lessons is a major problem for you, you could consider offering students a few minutes at the end of the lesson as a spontaneous reward for completing a task.

3. Use peer pressure

Set up an agreement with students whereby they can have, for example, an early finish, extra breaktime, computer access or a video show in return for losing five minutes of this preferred activity time every time a phone is heard, seen or used in class. Anyone violating the rule will make themselves very unpopular.

4. Encourage the use of phones as learning tools

Mobile phones now have hundreds of applications which can be effectively used to enhance education. While most state schools don't allow mobile devices because they are considered distractions, some schools and teachers have started to put the technology to positive use and this (quite surprisingly) seems to have led to a decline in inappropriate phone use during lessons.

At the most basic level a mobile phone can provide a basic suite of useful classroom tools. A class full of mobile phones means there is a complete set of calculators and stopwatches right there that can be used without a need for explanation and without much risk of any being stolen or lost. Most phones have cameras, so while in the past students always had to draw diagrams to show their scientific method and to record evidence, they can now take a photo instead. It gives them something that they can put straight into a report.

Text messaging provides a means of communication which is immediate, easy to use and preferred by students. Sending regular reminders to students by text message will be better received and less likely to be viewed as 'nagging' than face-to-face instruction which some students dislike. If it will help to engage a difficult student or encourage a shy one to participate, why not utilise the technology?

Here are some quick ideas for using mobile phones as learning tools in your school:

- Timing experiments with a stopwatch.

- Photographing apparatus and results of experiments for reports.

- Photographing texts/whiteboards for future review.

- Texting/emailing project material between group members.

- Receiving text and email reminders from teachers.

- Recording a teacher giving instructions or a tutorial for revision.

- Creating short narrative films using video.

- Downloading, listening to and translating foreign language podcasts.

- Answering questions delivered via podcasts.

- Using GPS to identify locations.

- Translating information into 'text speak' (or asking students to translate information into text speak as part of a review exercise).

- Using texts to pass on information for discussion.

- Using texts to answer questions in a quiz by texting the answer to an email address or phone.

- Sending random questions to class members.

- As an end-of-lesson review activity – students record the key points learned by voice or text and then save them in a suitable folder on their phones or text them to each other.

- Planning world domination (iPhone apps are available for this one in the iTunes store).

Dealing with students who won't complete homework

Getting students to complete homework is a common problem, especially with students who lack motivation. If they are not working in class where we can stand over them, they certainly aren't going to work at home. Here are six ways to encourage students to complete and return their homework – and none of them involve you dishing out a never ending stream of detentions or making promises of certificates and other treats (aka bribes!).

Make sure the work appeals to them

It sounds obvious but the more appealing you can make your homework in terms of having sufficient challenge, interest and practical value, the more chance your students will attempt it. With competition from television, games, friends and social media, if they see no point in it or if it's too boring/dull/easy, it's obviously not going to appeal. As a long term strategy, if students gain a sense of pride and accomplishment when they finish work, they are more likely to attempt future tasks.

Make it achievable

Ideally homework should be continuation of class work (rather than introducing something new) so they know how to do it. They need to know exactly what they are aiming for and what the finished product should look like. There is no point in giving them something they haven't got a clue about – it just won't get done.

Include an element of choice

Choice is an incredibly powerful motivator so it should be included in homework tasks. Give them a choice of task (e.g. Choose any three tasks from the following five …) or a choice in the presentation method (e.g. Produce a mindmap, report, illustration, magazine article or model to show …).

 You can download a collection of creative homework assignments from: www.noisyclass.com/bookresources.

Write it down

Always make sure students have the task (and any helpful instructions) written down clearly before they leave the room, or post the task up on a blog/website so they can access it any time. It cuts out the 'I didn't know what to do' excuses and provides them with a reminder should they get stuck.

Include group interaction

We know that students like to work together so there is some merit in the idea of occasionally (or even regularly if it proves successful) setting a project which requires students to work in groups. The individual accountability from peers involved in group work gives extra impetus to get the task completed.

Get parents/guardians involved

If you have children you're no doubt fully aware how much of a problem the whole issue of homework can cause at home. Parents do the cajoling, reminding, threatening, punishing and bribing, while kids do the lying, avoiding, promising, making excuses and delaying.

In many homes World War III breaks out over this single issue almost every night, while in others it isn't even mentioned. With this in mind, many parents/guardians (even those who appear totally unsupportive) will welcome help and direction from the school on the subject of homework and this can be a very effective way of gaining their support in return.

If you have trouble getting back-up from some parents, the key is to convince them that you are trying to help them and their child and make life easier for all. You don't want to come across as if this is for your benefit or to meet school targets; rather it's to help their child progress, succeed and do well. You need to show them how a little bit of support from them is going to have a dramatic effect on their child's progress in school and consequently on home life – happier child, easier life, fewer arguments, fewer detentions and fewer requests to visit school for a 'little chat'.

Begin by explaining to parents that homework involves the efforts of three separate parties – school, student, home – and that each party is dependent on support and input from the other two if the system is to work properly. Show them a record of any homework tasks that have been missed and explain the school policy and procedure for dealing with missed homework – adding that it is neither pleasant nor beneficial for the student. If possible, show them statistics for the effect of missed homework on overall grades.

Then describe specific things they can do to help, together with the days/times when this should happen. They will need a copy of the homework schedule showing the days the work has to be handed in together with the suggested time to be spent on a task. Setting a regular, definite block of time – say 4.30–5.30 p.m. – helps to teach students time management skills.

Try to encourage parents to set a time early on in the evening so that the child is still fairly alert and *The X Factor* hasn't started. The idea is to create a habit/routine which doesn't interfere with evening entertainment too much. Another reason to set an early time is that it enables consequences to be brought into play. If homework is set for last thing at night, and the child is allowed to play on their computer or watch TV all night before that, how can consequences be applied?

Parents will need a list of necessary materials and supplies to use at home. In some cases the school could supply these – you could even provide them with a set of 'parent notes' for a task the student is likely to find challenging so that they can take part and provide some assistance and instruction. I've dealt with many parents with severe academic limitations and they were delighted when I gave them these.

Finally, parents may benefit from some behaviour management guidance in terms of suitable consequences (e.g. withholding mobile phone, TV/computer game time, pocket money until homework is completed). The easier you can make it for them to get involved, the better the chances they will participate. In my experience, parents enjoy spending quality time with a child they have possibly had very little quiet contact with for a long time, so the students start to enjoy increased parental contact/attention as well as a sense of achievement.

 You can download a letter to parents template together with ten tips for parents to help with homework from: www.noisyclass.com/bookresources.

Dealing with students who don't bring equipment to class

Students not having the right equipment is one of those seemingly unimportant management issues which is often swept under the carpet by a teacher who is frantically trying to concentrate efforts on more serious problems. In a lively class, when you've got Chantelle and Courtney cat fighting, Liam smoking, Carl spitting on Connor, Kieron chucking textbooks at Jonny and Jonny making lewd comments about the support assistant's chest – all at the same time – it's easy just to hand a spare pen to Kyle who's forgotten his. After all, there is no need to get in a lather over the small stuff. Is there?

One reason we should be at least a little concerned about Kyle's missing pen is that seemingly trivial things like this can easily trip up the most well-prepared classroom manager if they get out of hand. Why? Because whatever you allow to happen in class, you effectively encourage.

Every time you hand over a pen from your dwindling pile of spares, you effectively train your little angels in the belief that it's perfectly acceptable to come to class without one. So before long, they are all at it. Suddenly, one pen becomes 35, you spend half the lesson handing pens out like sweeties and you're left with a handful of chewed biros and a group of kids who couldn't give two hoots about coming to class prepared.

The bottom line is that you want to minimise the number of excuses that students will have for not starting work. Let's face it, not having a pen is a great excuse to avoid transferring words onto paper, not having a ruler is a convenient pretext to avoid measuring or drawing straight lines, not having coloured pens means you can't finish your illustrations and not having a compass makes it absolutely impossible to draw circles (and give the student in front of you impromptu body piercings).

The more time you spend sourcing, fetching, carrying and monitoring equipment and resources, the more stressful your lessons will be, the less time you'll have to support and manage your students, and the more dependent they will become. And that's before we take into account valuable textbooks and exercise books which are taken home and never seen again.

So let's get on top of this issue and make life easier for everyone. Here are some classroom management strategies for dealing with students who don't bring equipment to class.

Don't let textbooks and exercise books out of your sight

I'm sure there is some complex mathematical formula to explain the relationship between a student's general classroom behaviour and the likelihood that he or she will return a book once it has been taken home, but let's just say that with a challenging group it's not very likely at all. And it causes huge problems.

I remember being pretty lax when it came to taking my own exercise books home as a student – they just seemed to disappear once they entered the depths of my school bag, never to be seen again. I had a new exercise book in some lessons almost every week so by the end of term there were hundreds of little books with 'Robert Plevin' labels on them lying around in uncharted places, each containing about three pages of work. Maybe it's just (disorganised) boys, but it's a problem which needs solving if you don't want all your lessons turned upside down with cries of, 'Miss, I need a new book'.

Your best bet is not to let them take exercise books home in the first place and store them on a dedicated class shelf instead. Yes, I know you have to set homework but there is nothing wrong with giving them a separate folder/book/file specifically for homework. And *never* send textbooks home – that's what photocopiers are for.

Offer to lend the student some of your equipment in return for one of their shoes as collateral

This quick and very effective strategy was suggested to me by a primary school teacher at a party years ago and I have used it successfully in various classrooms throughout my career. There are going to be some strategies in this book which you won't feel comfortable about using, and this is probably one of them – purely because it can get very smelly in a hot classroom when half the students are minus their full complement of footwear! Having said that, it is a very effective way of making sure you get your equipment back at the end of the lesson. Though now I come to think of it, I do still have a large collection of odd Woolworths plastic trainers – for some reason they seemed to think that a new HB pencil was a fair swap.

Encourage them to borrow from each other

Borrowing from their classmates is preferable to having to continually dole out materials from your own stocks. Give a brief period of time at the start of the lesson for students to loan items from other members of the class. Be prepared to change strategy if they start removing each other's shoes.

Use the positive approach

With any classroom problem there are two ways of approaching it – reward positive behaviour or punish inappropriate behaviour. Rather than focusing on students who don't bring equipment, it might be better to reward those who do with spontaneous light hearted treats, such as a garishly decorated plastic pen or an antique Woolworths training shoe.

Focus on teaching the behaviour you want to see

This is my personal favourite. I'm a big fan of methods which develop independence (give a man a fish and all that), and the more you can lead your students towards becoming responsible, the easier your job will be. Give them a checklist to take home and fill in every morning with items they should bring to school. Then show them how to use the checklist as a memory aid ('Have a quick look through it in the morning and check off items as you add them to your bag').

Get parents/guardians involved

Inform parents that their child not bringing the right equipment to class is a source of great concern. Explain how it is impacting on their progress in other lessons and its importance as a life/employment skill. You could also mention that disorganised teenagers tend to lack the ability to move out of the parental home and often end up living there well into their thirties. That usually gets them listening! Show them the checklist you've created and ask them to remind the student each morning/evening to use it.

Provide a resource box

Always have a resource box of materials and equipment on your desk. Cut out the tendency for students to keep/borrow/forget to give back/steal your materials by having them clearly and boldly marked. Pink nail varnish tends to be a good deterrent if you're lending materials to boys.

Keep a clear record

A great way to impress students with the impact of their actions is to give them a clear picture of how significant a particular problem is. A chart provides an unambiguous record, for both teacher and student, of how many times materials have been forgotten. It also gives a definite starting point from which to improve: 'Nathan, you have forgotten your materials every day this week. Let's see if we can get one positive mark on the chart tomorrow, shall we?'

Dealing with latecomers and poor punctuality

Once you've used the filter method to settle the majority of the class, students arriving late can be disruptive. Here is a selection of strategies and creative ideas for preventing the problem of punctuality, plus a complete step-by-step plan for dealing with students arriving late.

Have clear rules and consequences in place

Students wandering into class late is a common problem, particularly as they get older, but you can do much to prevent it by having clear, consistent rules on punctuality backed up by cast iron consequences. Students need to know exactly what will happen if they are late and that consequences will be applied every time, regardless of the excuse the student uses.

Consequences can form part of a hierarchical plan – from the two minute follow-up (see page 61) to time made up after school and contact with parents for more serious cases, or they can be more humorous – such as inviting students who are not in their seats when the bell rings to go to the front of the room and sing a song. It puts a smile on everyone's face and starts the class in an upbeat way. A colleague who favoured the humorous approach told me that when two students wandered in late she would have them sing a duet – and occasionally she even had a choir! She found that punctuality ceased to be an issue when she started using this strategy.

Reward those who are on time

Students like to do well and good attendance is something that all of them can achieve, regardless of ability, so it should be acknowledged like any other social skill. Recognition can take the form of verbal or written praise, a special award or more formal rewards such as free time.

Surprise, surprise!

Punctuality and attendance can be encouraged in a fun way by randomly choosing one student's desk or chair each day and placing a sticker or note beneath it. The student who arrives (on time) to find the sticker under his or her seat gets to choose a small prize. If the student is absent or late the prize is forfeited or cancelled.

Here is a step-by-step classroom management plan for dealing with latecomers:

- Give latecomers as little attention as possible. Calmly, and without fuss, take their name (assuming you don't already know it) and confirm that they are late: 'John, you're ten minutes late ...'

- Direct them to their seat. Quickly get them seated and give them something to occupy them – they could watch the remainder of an explanation/demonstration or get on with a worksheet or written task while you concentrate on the other learners.

- Don't ask them why they are late at this stage. This will cause disruption to the lesson flow and shift focus where you don't want it. They will be given opportunity to explain their reason for being late in the two minute follow-up after the lesson: 'Sit there please and get on with (insert task) – you can explain why you're late after the lesson.'

- Address latecomers separately once the other students are settled. Once the majority of the students are working the next step is to get the latecomer(s) engaged properly in the lesson task. This can be done either by gathering them as one group and giving them the full demonstration/

lesson introduction again or (better) pair them up with other students who can teach them or explain the task to them.

- Praise those who are working. Take the focus off the latecomer by giving positive attention to those who are working: 'Excellent work you two – nice to see you getting on with that.'

- Keep thorough records. Get latecomers to fill in a form giving the time they arrived and a reason for their late arrival. Send copies home with notification of consequences if it continues.

- If students are absent when worksheets are distributed place copies in folders for absentees. At the end of the day, simply label each folder with the absent students' names so that missed work is ready for their return.

Dealing with angry students – how to defuse arguments and confrontation

That said, here are some ways to deal with students when they become argumentative and confrontational.

Remain detached and keep calm

Remember that defiant behaviour is often a cry for help or an attempt to cover up a fear of failure. Nobody wants to look stupid in front of others (except those in the audition stages of *The X Factor*) and arguing against authority can be an effective distraction and a way of avoiding looking foolish. Being sensitive to your students' needs and the reasons behind their behaviour, rather than assuming they are being belligerent, makes it less likely that you will do or say something that will aggravate the situation and make matters worse. Remember also that their behaviour is most probably not aimed at you so try not to appear to take it personally.

Remove audience pressure

Some students will try to escalate the incident in front of their peers. If possible, speak to the student privately or redirect them and deal with the problem later: 'Let's not talk about it here – it could be embarrassing for both of us. Come and see me at lunchtime so that you can tell me everything that's bothering you – and come early so that you still get your break.' If they continue to argue, try any or all of the techniques listed here.

Divert their attention away from the incident/issue

If they continue to argue, try diverting their attention away from the incident/issue. Any form of distraction, such as asking them an off topic question ('Hey, I heard you were picked for the football team this week') or diverting them towards a new activity/scene ('Come and have a look at this over here') can switch their attention, take the heat out of a situation and provide the necessary change diversion.

Quite innocently, I once responded to a very irate, tantrum throwing teenage boy with the question, 'What colour are your socks?' His change in state was immediate and the expression on his face shifted from wild eyed fury to utter bewilderment as he stood, puzzled, looking at me. His mood was transformed and we both fell about laughing. 'What colour are your socks?' (or an equally random question) is now my standard response to anyone displaying a hissy-fit.

Do nothing

One of the best ways to get someone who wants an argument to stop, think and reflect on their behaviour is to deny them a reaction of any kind so the idea here is simply not to react: say and do nothing. Silence is very powerful at times like this. The student wants a response and by meeting them with an impassive look and total silence you clearly convey that you are in control and will not be drawn into an argument.

Be the one to back down

Say: 'Neither of us really want this to escalate so I'm going to leave it there. We can talk about it later if you want.'

Offer them space

Say: 'I don't want you to leave but equally I don't want things to get out of control. If you need to leave the room and compose yourself, I understand – there's the door. You can come back when you're ready.'

Take the 'one-down' position

Agree with them or apologise – it's a great disarmer: 'I think you're right. You've made me think that maybe I am a little bit too bossy sometimes. Will you accept my apology so we can start again?'

Ask for their help or advice

Asking students for help catches them completely off guard, immediately changes their negative state and can, more than any other technique I've tried, disarm the angriest of teenagers and get them on side. We all, on some deep level, like to feel needed and this is the easiest way of tapping into this primitive human trait.

> John, I know you're very good with technical equipment – please can you help me set up the AV equipment? We can talk about your homework after that.

> Simon, I've got a bit of a problem. My son is really struggling with one of his teachers at school. You remind me of him and I'm impressed with the way you've managed to turn yourself around over the last few months. Can you give me some advice to pass on to him?

How to start over with an impossible group

If you have reached the point where every lesson is a battle from bell to bell, where the group is totally against you and the A-Team is busy righting wrongs elsewhere, it's time for dramatic action.

With an extremely difficult group behaviours can become entrenched. The whole group gets used to fighting with the teacher (and each other) and destroying lessons becomes something of a game to them. On these terms, the lessons are a nightmare for the teacher and any attempt to take control is met with abuse, laughter or mockery.

One way to break this routine is to take charge through tough discipline – take the group back out and don't even let them into the room until control is established. Have a series of stepped consequences in place and follow up on each and every miscreant. This takes confidence – not only in oneself but also in the school system and support channels.

The clean slate (explained below) is an alternative way of breaking this negative pattern. I've used it many times and it has always worked, but caution is required – you will get a feel for the type of group this will work with. Attention-seekers, childish, silly and generally very difficult groups will like the clean slate and respond well to it straight away. The very rare 'nasties' (actually very rare indeed) will try to prevent you from completing the session. If they succeed, don't try this again – you only get one chance at the clean slate.

Do remember that it is often the most challenging groups that present the greatest opportunities in education. Turning these difficult but vulnerable young people around can be the most rewarding experiences of your career.

Here's how to break the habitual cycle of negativity and get this group on side with the 'clean slate'.

 ## The clean slate

Step 1: Break their routine

First you need some light refreshments – a few bargain bags of crisps, biscuits, some cordial and plastic cups as a minimum. The more you can turn this into a 'special occasion' the better – some background music (their choice of music ideally, not yours) would definitely help. The health-conscious might prefer fruit, nuts, wheatgrass and whale tunes.

Plonk the goodies on a table at the front and say something along the lines of:

> We need to start afresh. I'm concerned that you're all missing out. We can't go on as we have been so I'm hoping you'll join me to try to find a way forward over some snacks.

> The reason I'm here is to help you. I can't help you when we are fighting and I feel bad that I'm being paid for a job that I'm not able to do. It's not fair on you, it's not fair on your parents and it's not fair on me.

None of us are getting any benefit from this because I know each of you deep down wants the best for your life, and I'm hoping we can work together so that you might get something positive from our time together.

So ... this is your opportunity to tell me what you want from these lessons.

This approach catches the difficult group completely off guard; they don't expect it and it signals that you are prepared to use extreme measures to reach them. That in itself usually starts to get some attention, and even a little respect, from the most challenging students. Explain that their feedback and opinions will be used to compile a new set of rules for the classroom, a summary of which could also be sent out to parents.

Step 2: Group discussion

Ideally students should be seated in a circle or around one large table with one student acting as 'scribe' to record answers and points raised as you work through the following questions:

- What's working well – what do you like about our lessons?

- What's not working – what don't you like about our lessons?

- How can we improve as a group?

- What do you want to see more of? What sort of activities do you want?

- Are there other things we can change?

Note: Before starting the discussion, make sure the ground rules are clearly explained and displayed for all to see, and have stepped consequences in place for students who violate the rules. For example:

Discussion rules:

- No put-downs.

- Raise your hand to speak.

- You can speak when you've got the ball (have a ball or similar object which is passed around the group whenever anyone wants to talk).

- Listen to each speaker without interrupting – everyone has a right to be heard.

- Keep hands and feet to yourselves.

Consequences:

- Stage 1: Five minutes sitting out of the discussion in the classroom.

- Stage 2: Five minutes sitting outside the classroom.

- Stage 3: Parking in another class.

Don't rush through the discussion points – take them one at a time and try to get students to give as much feedback as possible on each point. For example, 'What don't you like about our lessons?' needs to be fully explored to get students to detail all the factors that they are finding disagreeable.

Some students will almost certainly tell you that they don't actually like the fact that there is so much noise (deep down all students want to do well). This then allows further discussion on the necessity for rules and consequences. Eventually, their feedback can be used to create a new set of class rules, so this stage of getting them to see the value of rules is essential.

In order to fully explore this issue you might ask, 'What would happen in a classroom without rules?' Or use analogies such as playing football or driving on a road: 'What would happen if there was no referee/no rules?' or 'What would happen if there were no traffic lights/road markings?'

Step 3: Follow-up session

After the discussion, compile their feedback into a summary sheet consisting of three to five new rules (based on what they felt was wrong with lessons) together with a list of things they would like you to include/exclude in lessons from now on (i.e. specific activities they like/don't like). Talk through the summary sheet to iron out any conflicts and then have each student sign a copy as a contract for future lesson behaviour.

Conclusion:
The end of the lesson

So we've come to the end of the lesson. By now we have our routines and classroom management essentials in place and we've explored strategies to deal with specific disruptions. The teacher knows exactly what she wants the students to do next – get cleared away as quickly as possible. So she gives the instruction to do so.

But which of these instructions is going to give her the greatest chance of success? (And if the correct answer isn't obvious by now, go and sit at the back of the class.)

(a) The bell is about to ring, everyone. Put everything away and get ready to be dismissed please … Come on everyone … Quickly now … Let's get packed away … *Hurry up!*

(b) Okay everyone, the bell is going to go in five minutes – it's time to clear away. You know what to do.

After giving instruction (b) the teacher then points to a printed routine, clearly displayed on the wall at the front of the room:

End of lesson routine

1. Put all textbooks on the shelf and exercise books on my desk.

2. Put all equipment away in the correct drawer or cupboard.

3. Clear your work area and sit silently facing the front.

4. After you get permission to leave, push in your chair and leave in silence.

5. If it is the last period of the day, stack the chairs by the back wall.

Vague instructions such as those in (a) more often than not lead to misbehaviour because they don't give the students clear enough direction. They will wander, play dumb, claim they didn't hear the bell and protest that they don't know where things are supposed to go. What should be a simple job quickly degenerates into a time consuming struggle in which you find yourself repeating instructions, shouting, yelling and having to deal with one avoidance tactic after another.

Instruction (b) works because the teacher has already spent time teaching her students a clear routine for the end of the lesson. There is no need for confusion or wasted time. No need to repeat instructions. No need to check that everyone has understood or give extra prompts to those who haven't. Everyone knows exactly what to do and the teacher is free to oversee the whole process with little need for involvement or intervention.

So, that's it. With the strategies we've explored hopefully you are feeling in control and ready for your next class.

 You can download a full set of ready-made routines from: www. noisyclass.com/bookresources.

List of strategies

The number one secret to effective classroom management

Positive reinforcement

Taking control at the door

Seating plans

Getting them into the room – the filter method

Getting the lesson started

Maintaining a positive learning environment

Maintaining lesson flow

Dealing with problems

Made in United States
North Haven, CT
06 September 2022